HEALING
– MORE OR LESS

Frontispiece by PETER PELZ

Christ embracing the sufferer with Kaposi's Sarcoma

HEALING
– MORE OR LESS

❖❖❖❖❖❖❖❖❖❖❖❖❖❖❖❖❖❖❖❖❖❖❖❖❖❖❖❖

Reflections and prayers
on the meaning and ministry of healing
at the end of an age

JIM COTTER

SHEFFIELD
CAIRNS PUBLICATIONS
1990

First published 1987
Second edition 1990

Further copies of this book are obtainable from
Cairns Publications
47 Firth Park Avenue, Sheffield S5 6HF

CONTENTS

PREFACE

THIS book of reflections and prayers has been shaped by two concerns. In religious circles, the word 'healing' is often given too narrow a meaning, that of a miraculous moment of physical cure. Though such an emphasis is likely in a time of bewildering and frightening change, these meditations seek to range more widely and deeply. For the individual there is a lifetime to consider: healing is not confined to specific incidents or occasions of prayer. And there is the health and well-being of the body politic to consider, from the local community to the planet itself. All these concerns are intimately connected. More than ever no one of us is an island. And we need to look widely and steadily precisely because our vision is liable to contract in fearful times.

The second concern is to challenge the view that physical health is of little importance in the perspective of eternity, that it doesn't really matter if you are dying out of due time because life after death is going to be much better than on earth. Now it is true that Christian belief does not confine life to this world, ultimately including death and going beyond it, but a healthy flesh-body and the well-being of a community are both real, if partial, signs of the Commonwealth of God. They are samples, firstfruits, of what shall be, and to be genuinely affirmed as such. So a Christian concern for healing must range beyond the specifically religious confines of prayer and church. And when the whole of life on this planet seems in mortal danger, it is particularly tempting to think only of ourselves and to project contentment into a life beyond death. Again we need to look widely and steadily: we must refuse to narrow our vision of a transformed earth just because the challenge seems beyond us.

There is one disease in particular which is alerting us to these concerns. Miracles are few (if any), and we want to turn away from those afflicted. And that disease – more accurately syndrome – is AIDS. It is much easier to offer a better life after death than to live and die with AIDS openly and well, either carrying the virus ourselves or including an awareness of it and drawing close to those who carry it.

AIDS demonstrates that disease cannot be separated from the social, political, and moral dimensions of the life of a community, nor from the deep-seated irrational ways in which we can all at times react to such illnesses. Associations with sex and blood make such reactions even more intense. Add to this the fact of a condition that is incurable, the fact that a virus can be passed invisibly from person to person, and the fact that many young people are dying, and it is no wonder that we have a crisis on our hands, one that challenges our capacity to care and that mercilessly exposes the weaknesses of our faith.

Chapter 5 in this book tries to let the particularities of this crisis concentrate the mind and heart, so that we might find sober encouragement and hope. The frontispiece by Peter Pelz, to whom I am grateful for permission to use it, shows a Christ-figure holding a man suffering from one of the opportunistic diseases of AIDS, the skin cancer, Kaposi's sarcoma.

I am also grateful to several people whose thinking has helped me over the years and whose ideas have become woven into my own. I want especially to acknowledge the writings of John V. Taylor and Michael Wilson, the prayer books of the Church of England and the Episcopal Church of the United States, and the publications of the Guild of Health. The section on anointing with oil is indebted to a conversation with Alan Harrison, to whom I am also grateful for one of the Forewords. I thank Norry McCurry for the other.

I should also like to acknowledge with appreciation the people of the parish of All Saints', Leavesden, Watford, whose stimulus led to the publication of the first edition of this book.

The last three chapters and the first two appendices include material for corporate and individual prayer for healing. I have included it as a resource to be drawn upon for various occasions, not as a ready-made order of service. And imaginative use will mean that alterations will soon be made to what is printed here. These particular words are not sacrosanct. But the author would appreciate the courtesy in use, if there are substantial alterations, of acknowledging both original source and the changes made.

In one or two places I have used material from other books of my own compilation, *Prayer at Night* and *Through Desert Places: A version of Psalms* 1–50, and from *By Stony Paths: A version of Psalms* 51–100, which is due to be published in 1991.

One particular note of explanation: 'Bapu' is an eastern word for 'Father', and in its context (and, I think, in its sound) combines respect with intimacy. It seems to me that this is the note we need to internalize when we address God as Father, rather than the one of childish dependence.

Appendix B is based on a ritual devised by Bernice Broggio and Teresa Parker, and I'm grateful for their permission to use and amend it. I also thank Gill Butt and Mary Robins for their comments on the draft.

When the first edition of this book was launched on 8 April 1987, it was accompanied by a lecture that was subsequently issued as a pamphlet, *What price healing in a time of epidemic?* Though there is some overlap with the reflections in chapter 5 of the book, it seems appropriate to include it, with some amendments, as an appendix to this edition. It was dedicated at the time – a dedication I wish to renew here – to Bill Kirkpatrick and Bernard Lynch, Anglican and Roman Catholic priests respectively, both of whom have shown me and many others, in their response to those who are suffering from AIDS, what it is to bear the cost of compassion, and who have given of themselves more than their fair share, in the maelstroms of London and New York.

There was a third dedication made only on the occasion itself. That was to my father, who even in the last days of his fading, offered to do anything he could through prayer and counsel to help those suffering from AIDS. He had died but two days previously, 6 April 1987.

Only a few weeks ago I was talking with a woman who had been in a youth group that my father led forty years ago. She remembered that they had known that whatever they might do he would not have ceased to love them. If that is the image of God that we seek to embody, then we shall indeed be both carriers of the meaning and bearers of the ministry of healing.

JIM COTTER
Sheffield, March 1990

FOREWORDS

THE Introduction, 'Concerning the Service of the Church', to the 1662 Book of Common Prayer complains that previously "to turn the Book only was so hard and intricate a matter, that many times there was more business to find out what should be read, than to read it when it was found out." The same could be said today about the proliferation of books on, and the liturgical expression of, the Churches' Ministry of Healing. There were times during my Chaplaincy to the Guild of Health when I felt the first thing in need of healing was the ministry of healing. Why is it that a ministry devoted to promoting that which Christ promised ("I am come that they might have life and have it in its fulness") too frequently becomes divisive and the source of so much pettiness and empire building?

Yet things are changing. Searching and radical questions are being asked. Francis MacNutt in his book, *Healing,* asks if what is at stake in the religious healing movement is our view of the nature of God. Stephen Pattison in his book *Alive and Kicking* says that illness is a mystery which eludes all our attempts at comprehension and control. When it is presented or dealt with in a simple or one-sided way by healers of any kind, secular or religious, we can be fairly sure that it is being misrepresented. Early Christian attitudes to illness recognized that it could come from divine, evil, or natural sources. The important thing is to discern the wider purpose and meaning of the illness rather than simply trying to eradicate it, for God might be trying to communicate something through it.

In 1987 Jim Cotter published the first edition of this book of reflections and prayers, *Healing – More or Less,* which highlighted all this in a practical and prayerful way, in an attempt to open up yet further our understanding of this ministry. The very title underlines the need to discern God's purpose and what is being communicated. This new and revised edition takes us a further step with more reflections, a deeper understanding of the Psalms, and the facing of the fact that there

xi

is no one correct way of looking at illness. There are many different and helpful ways of thinking about it in the world today.

ALAN HARRISON
Goring, June 1990

IT is the rite for anointing with oil in this book which I continue to find of value in my ministry as a spiritual director and retreat conductor, for I have grown to believe increasingly in the sacramental value of holy oil – and not only for the sick.

The traditional and contemporary liturgical forms have a certain dullness, and we need words which draw out the power of what is happening. Jim Cotter uses images which are bold and imaginative, and I have many times felt grateful for his book.

He traces the action of God in joyful lyrical terms which are full of energy, and I have used the prayers regularly to anoint retreatants as they go into the world. Anointing seals what they have received and commissions them for what lies ahead.

NORRY MCCURRY
London, July 1990

I
More than cure

I. A HEALTHY PERSON

THE whole of me, the whole person,
physical, mental, emotional, spiritual,
is in need of being healed,
of being made whole.
The curing of physical symptoms
is but one part of this process:
the absence of cure need not hinder it.

Illness is not an unfortunate incident,
but a phase of life with its own time and meaning.

The words 'healing' and 'salvation' are close:
they derive from the same Greek root, 'sozein'.
We experience moments of salvation,
the gift and the grace of freedom,
of breathing again in wide open spaces,
of being sprung from the trap,
released from confinement or oppression.

My own healing is bound up with that of others.
I need to pray and work
for the healing of the nations,
for food for the hungry,
for justice for the downtrodden,
for my neighbours in a global village.
Without their well-being
I cannot be completely well.

Everything that I am and do
contributes to the making of my soul-body,
and the making of the soul-bodies of others,
and the coming to glory of the whole universe.
The eye of faith looks to a transfiguration
of everything that is of agony or ecstasy
in the life of my flesh-body,
of the flesh-bodies of others,
of the material stuff of this earth and beyond.

Through grace and in faith
I receive the gift of eternal life,
abiding close to the self-giving love of God,
the love that is not destroyed by death.

II. A HEALTHY COMMUNITY

WE are not afraid of differences,
rather are we enriched by them.

We do not turn away from disabilities,
distancing ourselves through fear,
but we draw near and touch,
and wrestle with whatever keeps us,
visibly or invisibly handicapped,
from loving one another to completion.

We recognize how the illness of an individual
so often reflects a corporate dis-ease in society:
pollution, radiation, working conditions, city stress.

We soberly remember that we are relatively well
at other people's expense.

We do *not* desire one single good
to the exclusion of other goods.
We do not exaggerate the significance of
one particular expensive treatment or piece of research.
We do not embrace one single cause
with excessive and exclusive zeal.
This would be to act in the spirit of pride, of hubris,
of claiming value at the expense of the unnoticed.

We spend more on education for health
than on glamorous technological projects.

We approach death as a kindly boundary to earthly life,
giving that life both challenge and measure.

III. A HEALTHY WORLD

A WORLD in which we know deeply
that we belong to one another:
there is no place of escape from
those who are tiresome,
those from whom we draw back.

A world in which we pray and work
for the well-being of business, factory, farm, bank,
where we search together for meaning and purpose,
where we repent of what goes wrong between us,
where we act to put things right,
where we celebrate what goes well.

A world in which we are alert to signs of God
at work in the way things are being done,
God striving through us to transform
the realms of this world
into the realm of Christ.

A world in which the contribution
of those who work in public health,
in waterworks, sewage farms, civil engineering,
is valued and held in high esteem.

A world flowing with milk and honey,
with corn and wine and oil,
where salvation is known to be
not less than freedom from deprivation.

A world in which there is sensitivity
towards those who have less than little,
a world in which there is action together
to ensure that all have clean water,
adequate food,
a place to live,
and the opportunity to contribute
to the common good.

A world in which we take corporate action
to challenge and change evil ways
in the policies and practice of corporate bodies
that destroy, deprive, and pollute.

A world in which we care for
the air and water,
the soil and trees,
of the planet we share,
our common earth home.

A world in which nations maturely handle
large-scale changes to eliminate poverty,
changes that are political, economic, military.

A world where we become more healed
by being prepared to bear more
for the sake of those who are less well.

"Is not this the fast that I choose:
to loose the bonds of wickedness,
to undo the thongs of the yoke,
to let the oppressed go free,
and to break every prison bar?

"Is it not to share your bread with the hungry,
and bring the homeless poor into your house;
when you see the naked to cover him,
and not to hide yourself from your own flesh?

"Then shall your light break forth like the dawn,
and your healing shall spring up speedily."

[*Isaiah* 58.6–8]

"The kingdom of the world
has become the kingdom of our Lord and of his Christ,
and he shall reign for ever and ever."

[*Revelation* 11.15b]

2
A symbol of something more

THE healings of Jesus were
symbols,
parables of much more than cure,
indicators of the way God wills life to be,
heralds of a new age,
events that raised questions:

Do you want to become a more responsible person,
and if so, do you really *want* to be healed?

Do you need to know that you are forgiven?

Is the spirit of trust growing in you –
and in your friends, who may, in faith,
carry you when you are too weak to know or care?

Can you let go of fear and doubt and resentment,
can you bear sorrow and decay,
in the light of a belief
that death is not the final power?

However raw your life
and however much pain you bear,
can you use this very raw material
to allow God to shape you,
not for ease, but for glory?

7

Is your life about being physically well and sleek,
or is your first priority being Christlike –
humble, grateful, trusting, forgiving?

II. UNUSUAL HEALINGS NOW

AN unusual healing evokes wonder:
"It was so unexpected, such a surprise,
it filled me with joy and gratitude:
it was a miracle."
So says the person suddenly cured of a disease,
so says the woman who gives birth after years of hoping.

Let our response be thankfulness to God,
and a deepening of our faith and trust,
and prayer that such events become more everyday.

And let us also reflect –

Much in life that cannot now be explained
may be understood in years to come.

God is as much to be praised in the commonplace
as in the unusual,
in the surgeon's skill as in the healer's hands.

Those with abilities that others cannot grasp,
like that of the accountant or the healer,
may use that gift either to exercise control,
and so boost a salary or a sense of self-importance,
and in the process dominating others,
or to serve the good of others
and so build up the community.

Even after a marvellous cure,
there are challenges to be faced:
the healing of the whole personality,
and of broken or partial relationships,
is a long, deep, and costly process.
Faith in God through it all is never easy
and grace is not cheap.

We are always being tempted to give up responsibility,
give power into the hands of others.
If we need help because we are in pain,
we will all too easily give the doctor complete power,
and say to our friends, 'Doctors' orders.'
We will cast our troubles in the mould
we think the expert expects –
and sometimes does so expect –
the specialist, the exorcist, the therapist,
complying with their world view.
So we may seek healing
but by means of lying and pretence.

Dramatic healings can easily be misunderstood.
Jesus himself saw the temptation of using power
to stun people into following him unthinkingly.
"Turn stones into bread...
throw yourself off the Temple roof..."
And he realized that deep and lasting healing
comes only through struggle, weakness, suffering, death.
The way of amazing power is too shallow.

3
Powers yet to be shaped

I. TO EXCLUDE?

So often we *fight* disease.
In thinking thus we are using the language of conflict,
the language of banishment, exclusion, casting out.
We talk of heart *attacks,*
invading bacteria,
being *laid low* by a virus,
anti-biotics,
bombardment with rays,
in the grip of forces that cannot be controlled,
something *came over me.*

We need to be careful about such language:
it is all too easy to exclude what is inconvenient,
anything or anyone who makes us feel uneasy,
to assume that they must be banished or destroyed
just because they make us feel uncomfortable.
We project our fear on to a large screen,
and say that we don't want to see *them,*
whether they be the mentally handicapped, the elderly,
the disfigured, the person with AIDS.

But is not exclusion *at best* an *emergency* measure?

We amputate a leg only when necessary to save a life.

We imprison people because we know no more constructive way
of righting a personal and social relationship
that has gone wrong.

We used to remove parts of a person's brain
so as to stop certain patterns of behaviour.

We used to burn people at the stake
because of their supposed evil or heresy,
saying, 'This is for the good of your soul...'

II. TO DISTANCE?

SOMETIMES a distancing is necessary,
but for the sake of a deeper coming together later,
or for the sake of a greater maturity.
It can be for our good that we are apart.

Parents and children have to separate, for
"Selfhood begins with a walking away,
And love is proved in the letting go."
(C. Day Lewis)

Couples may need to separate
so that they can learn to grow out of a 'love'
that has been too much a possessing and being possessed.

Some prayers of 'exorcism' have helped a distancing,
for example between living and departed.
It is a prayer of letting go,
either by the living or by the ancestor.

Some are helped by visualizing a compulsion
as an 'entity' that can be commanded in the name of Christ
to leave a person and cause no more disturbance.

Externalizing may be a useful *temporary* tactic
in order the easier to understand and come to terms
with a wound within.

III. TO INCLUDE?

PRAYERS of exorcism may look beyond excluding or distancing
to the hope of reconciliation and inclusion. Two examples:

> In the name of Christ,
> I bid you depart, [N], and trouble us no more.
> Be taken up into the presence of God
> until such times as we can be reconciled.

> In the name of Christ,
> come out of darkness into light [N];
> help us to understand you,
> that we may know your name and nature,
> striving with you in the love of God,
> so that you may come to yield your energy
> in the service of all that is holy.

Yes, there is sometimes chaos inside a person.
But much 'devilish' behaviour occurs
because we have been deeply hurt and desire revenge.
We have not yet come to terms with the fact
that all of us hurt one another.
Especially do we hurt the very young and vulnerable.
And we do not yet realize that blame-throwing is of no use.

The challenge is to understand these threatening powers,
to forgive those who hurt us,
and to go through the pain of separation and loneliness,
rather than escape from it into compulsion and false solace.

If we so accept the challenge,
we shall emerge more whole,
compulsive behaviour will diminish.
Energy that has been bound will be released,
we shall be able to choose how to direct and shape it.
For the area of our freedom will have been enlarged.

Jesus did not escape *from* cruxifixion,
but went through it.
He did not expel the evil that came at him,
but absorbed and transformed it.
He *withstood, stood under, under-stood,*
enduring as seeing the One who is invisible.

We cannot banish to the 'desert'
that which is destructive and evil,
for in one very small world,
and one in which we connect in our inner lives,
maybe even across the generations,
there is no 'over there' to which to exile the other.
What is 'desert' to one is 'territory' to another.
Together we are challenged to tackle what is evil.

So often, too, we want to banish parts of ourselves,
so unwelcome to the part of us that is in control,
which seeks to put on a respectable and acceptable face.
We condemn and rage against the enemy within.
For a while we may succeed in keeping that enemy
out of our own sight and awareness.
Yet this so-called 'enemy' is our hidden, neglected self,
which is in need of our compassion and patient care,
of awareness, acceptance, and reconciliation.

IV. IN A NUCLEAR AGE

My pact with the Destroyer
was signed before my hands were old enough to hold the pen.

> "Deeply desiring that bonfire –
> detonated in the desert of the West
> in the Anno Domini of my birth –
> to spread and engulf a hated world,
> I relish my enemy's holocaust
> who is now my neighbour and myself."

"Nonsense, we all desire peace."

The desire denied yet haunts,
disturbs a dream,
urges in moment of pique,
a glimpse of prejudice
dismissed as trivial by the conscious mind.

The desire grows,
brushing past me
as I press a button
that draws a curtain
and consigns a corpse
to crematorium flames.

The desire reigns:
needle, pellet, trigger, button,
move closer to my reach.
I look into the Abyss,
see the reflection of my own self-loathing,
and cackle, "Welcome."

Simple, satisfying, Final Solution,
Auschwitz the curtain raiser
pales to insubstantial ash.

No longer do I say
"See you tomorrow, D.V."
Rather do I mutter to capricious gods,
"Presidents and Secretaries permitting."
I do not know if I will them
to protect or to destroy.

The pact cannot be unmade
until with clear-eyed courage
I dare to dive in dark grey seas,
muddied by an ancient turbulence,
dig out the parchment from the sand,
and let it rise.

I recognize the writing as my own,
unlimited evil in my bland suburban heart,
thirst for revenge against an unknown source of pain.
I weep the cleansing truth that *I* desire these things.

In quietness of tears spent,
I look again into the deep Abyss,
consign the parchment to the flames,
and see them form the Face
that holds me without words.

Marked indelibly by eyes of fierce compassion,
empowered and burning,
stripped of the sentimental mask of cruelty,
I walk in clear-eyed gentleness,
with firm and kindly tread on cared-for earth.

4
Bearing

BEARING ONE ANOTHER'S BURDENS

SOME people become voluntary pain-bearers,
absorbing the anger and hurt of others,
and giving back acceptance and care.

Think of the charge nurse on a hospital ward,
bearing the anxiety of the patient,
the panic of a mother whose son is in intensive care,
the stress of the staff.

Think of the therapist,
who for a while becomes the client's hated parent
and who receives the vengeful feelings of the betrayed child,
and does not give back further pain.

Think of those on the end of telephones –
the Samaritans listening to the despairing,
the complaints departments of a store or transport system
receiving the anger of the public.

Think of the 'buddy' who cares for the person with AIDS,
maybe one who has been rejected by family and friends.

These are the ones who refuse to blame-throw,
who refuse to scapegoat individuals or minority groups,
who bear the discomfort of a world far from well.

Go deeper still into what healing is about,
and you discover a strange yet creative exchange
among those who admit to each other
that they are wounded.
In the bearing of one another's burdens,
in the sharing of one another's pain,
we begin to dance.

When we visit the sick,
really visit,
being there for the other
with the whole of ourselves,
we find that we are visiting Christ.
To look into gaunt and hollow eyes,
full of pain and longing and courage,
is to look into the eyes of Christ.
Christ is the one who is ill,
the one whom we tend,
the one who is vulnerable to our blundering.

I sit by your side.
I have nothing to say.
There is nothing I can do.
I am anxious.
I am afraid.
But I stay.

You are the needy one.
You are in my power.
I can refuse to be with you.
I can reject you within myself.
Or I can be with you,
loving you,
gently touching you.
You challenge me to a choice.
You judge me.

Together we dance the dance of the crippled –
crippled, because, however fit and handsome,
we are all far from being truly whole;
nevertheless a dance
because in the midst of suffering
we give each other courage and joy.
Here is a sign that indeed one day
we shall be well
and all shall be well,
broken bones shall joy,
and with those very wounds
we shall find that we have been made whole.

"Surely he has borne our griefs
and carried our sorrows;
yet we esteemed him stricken,
smitten by God and afflicted.
But he was wounded for our transgressions,
he was bruised for our iniquities;
upon him was the chastisement that made us whole,
and with his stripes we are healed."

[*Isaiah* 53.4–5]

"Bear one another's burdens,
and so fulfil the law of Christ."
[*Galatians* 6.2]

"My sorrow cannot be healed,
I am sick at heart...
My heart has been crushed,
because my people are crushed.
Is there no balm in Gilead?
Are there no doctors there?
Why, then, have my people not been healed?
I wish my head were a well of tears,
so that I could cry day and night,
for my people who have been killed."

                    [*Jeremiah* 8.18, 21–8.1]

5
Bearing more

I. A LIFE-THREATENING EPIDEMIC

IT is a time of fear, of apprehension,
a fear of pain and disfigurement,
a fear of hateful eyes and deeds of violence,
a fear of the power of those who want
to quarantine, to imprison,
to tattoo with identity marks,
a fear of the death-dealing.
There is a tightening,
a pressure on the chest,
a gasping for air,
a desire for the open space
beyond the narrow constricted gate.
There is a cold fear in a time of tribulation,
a time of the olive press, the winepress,
the crushing of the grapes,
and no guarantee of a good vintage . . .

From the heart of suffering rise the ancient cries,
O God, why?
O God, how long?
O God, why so much pain?
Why these ever-repeated battles,
why these swathes cut through a generation?
Why this horrific sacrifice?
For what?
Why?

And the cry is met with silence.

Still I hammer at God,
snarling with rage,
sweating with fear,
spitting into that all-seeing eye,
shouting at ears that are deaf.

Yet again there is silence.

Dare we look at you, O Christ,
at a God involved in the isolation and despair,
a God willing to be contaminated, to be infected,
who loves faithfully, in patient endurance?
Will all that is being created
reach its final destiny
in glory, joy, and love?

That sounds all very well from a pulpit.
Down here it adds salt to the wound.
God, does the preacher limp?
If so, there is hope.
Keep hope alive in me.

II. AN APOCALYPTIC TIME

AN apocalyptic time is a time of crisis,
a time of judgment,
of discerning and discarding,
a time of sifting,
of making clear where people stand,
a time for choice.

There is no sign of deliverance at such a time,
no hope, no meaning: it is a day of the 'wrath'.
It is a time of eclipse, of not knowing,
of learning how to bear a new and impossible burden,
deeper and deeper within us and among us.

It is a time of being redeemed by fire or fire –
the fire that destroys, the fire that refines,
the fire that gives warmth and light?

Is not our present fear of nuclear annihilation,
either suddenly or by seeping radiation,
and our fear of poisoned air,
silent, invisible, all-pervasive,
being projected on to a virus and those who carry it?
Is not this at least part of the reason
for the excessive fear and panic?
Do we see a spreading of cancer of the skin
and also beyond it to the tracts of barren land,
to eroded soil and creeping deserts?
Do we hear the gasping of lungs
and also beyond them to the damaged forests and changing air?
Can we allow our terror to surface,
to be acknowledged,
to melt in the warmth of an invincible love,
and so to choose now to become a people
of unprecedented truth, candour, and trust?

III. AIDS A JUDGMENT ON US ALL

THE presence of AIDS in our midst demands a response.
It shows our attitudes clearly by forcing us to make choices:
the degree of our health is revealed by our response.

Do you punish or embrace a sufferer?

Do you isolate the other or do you care for the other?

Are feelings of condemnation evoked in you,
anger and violence on the loose in your unconscious,
repressed but bursting out when you least expect it,
and then projected on to those who are vulnerable?

Or have you let those feelings surface within you,
to be acknowledged and worked with,
so that out of your own struggle to become more whole
you can show compassion to those who are vulnerable?

Do you hate yourself the more
or do you know yourself more deeply loved?

Do you oversimplify
or do you bear the complex and the unresolved?

Do you exclude, quarantine, withdraw,
or do you include, draw near, touch, and hold?

Do you scapegoat the different
or do you welcome their unusual gifts?

Do you reject the disfigured and the dying
or do you sit with them in peaceful presence
and in silent prayer?

Do you find yourself drawing back, awkward and afraid,
or does your heart go out to those who suffer?

AIDS judges us all by the truth that there are limits –

We may believe we have a right to unlimited travel,
to ever-increasing mobility,
to make more and more acquaintances.
But where are the roots, the depth, the love?

We may believe we have a right to self-expression,
but how far, and at whose expense?

We may believe we have a right to more and more,
to transcend limits,
but who pays?
And what of our death-limited organism and planet?

We are judged by those who live with HIV,
who have courageously faced the truth of themselves,
who, without formal faith,
have nonetheless gone beyond the power of death,
who care more deeply than ever for one another,
and are intensely alive.

IV. FAITH'S ORDEAL

MANY will fall by the wayside in this crisis
through which the world is passing.
and for those who do fall,
maybe their only choice is how to fall,
afraid, rebellious, or trusting.

We are angry that such things should happen –
and yet we are aware of so little.
Faith may give us a glimpse
that we are part of a history
that we cannot completely understand,
a short story within a greater story,
a thread of an intricate tapestry.
But this gives us no easy certainty.
God does not automatically and immediately
make everything all right.
God does not intervene sporadically,
even as a *benevolent* puppeteer,
but lets be what goes wrong,
suffering and redeeming the consequences
in a love that never lets go.

So when everything is going wrong for us,
at a profound level – *in God* –
everything is all right.
Love does not let go –
never, never, never, never, never.

I find that conviction impossible to proclaim,
I can but whisper it.
I do not have the confidence of a century ago,
nor the ringing faith of
"*Firmly* I believe and truly," but...

V. BARELY I BELIEVE

BARELY I believe yet truly
God is One and God is Three,
God is Love and seen most fully
Hanging from the wintry Tree.

And I trust Creator Spirit
In and through our common life
Weaving threads all torn and broken,
Shaping justice out of strife.

And I cherish – with due patience –
For the sake of God alone,
Words and Folk of Inspiration,
And the Sacraments Christ's own.

I embrace the Law of Loving,
Dying to possessive need,
Risen with Christ, though crushed by winepress,
Into spacious glory breathed. (1)

VI. ENDURING THE LACK OF MEANING

"WE must accept the fact
that this is an age
in which the cloth is being unwoven.
It is therefore no good trying to patch.
We must, rather, set up the loom
on which coming generations may weave new cloth,
according to the pattern God provides."

                              Gilbert Shaw (2)

We need to beware of importing meaning into AIDS.
We want order, we want to make sense of what is happening.
But it is too easy to come to premature conclusions.
We oversimplify if we introduce familiar categories –
like religious doom, judgment, and punishment.
We do well to be tentative and to withhold judgment.
We have to live with the fact that we cannot yet –
and maybe we never shall be able to –
discern *any* meaning in this disease.

> I wouldn't know what to say.
> I knew him in his prime,
> lively, intelligent, witty, loving:
> it was a tonic just to be with him.
> He was eloquent too,
> even – and this is ironic – on the problem of suffering.

> > Now you can hardly recognize him.
> > and he can't speak.
> > A stroke was it? A virus? A tumour?
> > What does the label matter?
> > The *person* we loved,
> > the one we all looked up to,
> > is reduced to this...

> It seems so pointless: it *is* so pointless.
> Both of us are speechless.
> So much for the wisdom of old age,
> the elders sitting in the city square.
> This is the reality,
> incontinent and helpless in an oblong ward.

No meaning here, no purpose, no gain that we can see,
either for him, or for those who care for him.
Just this hard implacable *fact* of his suffering.
He's not hurting instead of someone else –
no courageous witness of the prison camp.
He's not hurting on behalf of others –
showing them that there's a way through.
Just useless, useless anguish . . .

'Useless' –
the word catches us out.
This is where we go wrong.
We are so attuned to the values of the age
that we judge only by results,
by usefulness.

No wonder we are rendered speechless
by any 'thusness' that will not budge.
We have no power to produce results.
"I'm afraid there's nothing more that we can do."
We interpret this as doom, as sentence of death.
But perhaps it is a sign,
this being utterly useless.

For if I'm loved in that precise condition,
not respected, not needed, not able to give,
then love might be, might be,
the power that moves the universe...

VII. DISEASE AND SIN

THERE is no straightforward connection
in terms of cause and effect
between acts of wrongdoing and disease.
But there *is* a connection.
Disease is one of the manifestations of 'sin',
if by sin we mean
the tendency of the whole of life to be organised
for decay, disaster, destruction, disfigurement, death,
together with the self-devouring desire for these things.

When we examine the context of our experience,
we do perceive some degree of connection
between sexual intercourse and certain diseases;
between coal mining and lung complaints;
between business stress and heart attacks;
between anxiety and ulcers;
between radiation and pollution and cancers.

There is no simple cause and effect,
but diseases are signs of a corporate gonewrongness –
or at least a not-yet-right-ness –
a pervasive disorientation in which we are all caught.
It is impossible, unhelpful, and cruel
to apportion individual blame,
but certain states of mind
and certain ways of acting
can make us more prone to certain kinds of disease.

If diseases are, as some would claim,
God's punishment, God's wrathful thunderbolts,
we have to admit that the targeting is inaccurate.
For drug traffickers and arms traders flourish,
lesbian women are least likely to contract AIDS,
and infants develop the symptoms of the syndrome.
Rather is it an illness – and perhaps sinful –
to revel in the thought of punishment or act upon it,
as though we were wise and just arbiters.
God makes the sun to rise on the evil and on the good,
and sends rain on the just and the unjust. (3)

God does not run the world by *our* ideas
of reward and punishment.
Health and vigour do *not* correlate well
with virtue and innocence.
and if health does not prove goodness,
affliction does not prove wickedness.

It is *we* who do the blaming of the 'victims'.
"The unemployed are lazy."
Did laziness increase dramatically in the eighties?
Was it more likely in northern England than in the south?
"The cancer patient chose to eat the wrong foods."
"The rape victim enticed the rapist."

      The trouble is we feel more secure
      when we try to shift the blame,
      and we bargain with God –
      "I'll keep the rules – be good to me."

All are in need of repentance, *without exception*.
No one is without sin, no one dare cast a stone.
The ones who are judged most severely in the Gospels
are the hypocritical, the self-righteous, the merciless.
Disease therefore is not a punishment,
but a challenge among the myriad opportunities of our lives
to make of those lives something more full and satisfying.

VIII. HOSTING A VIRUS?

WE belong to each other in an intimate way
when we exchange fluids, energy, material stuff.
If we do this too often, we may overdo it.
We may try to take in too much,
like trying to take in too much information,
or trying to get to know too many people.
The organism cannot cope:
it tries to expel 'foreign' matter
because there is too much to absorb, process, change.
The exposure may sometimes be too much for the system,
there may be an immune overload, and consequent breakdown.

      How much can we 'host', can we 'carry'?
      We bear within us much that is potentially lethal,
      including parasites and cancerous cells.
      Are we challenged to bear, to contain,
      even to care for and transform
      a minute entity in the life of the universe
      which is wild, retrograde, and 'on the loose'?

It may be that those most fitted to be 'hosts',
who come to an 'accommodation' with the virus,
will prove to be those most fitted to survive.
We may do well to connect this 'hosting'
to a range of issues of health and well-being,
such as diet, physical movement, relaxation,
meditation, contemplation, sensitizing of touch.

If I have to carry you for the rest of my life,
if I am to be a carrier, a bearer, a host,
accepting you as part of the burden of the world,
then I must let no attitude or action of mine
encourage your urge and power to destroy
at the biochemical cellular level of the organism
that is my flesh-body self.

If each person is a universe in miniature,
you, and viruses like you,
may be in each of us always.
However much you are held at bay,
your power of destruction lurks,
We cannot expel, conquer, defeat, or destroy you.
We belong together,
we die or live together,
are bound hellward or heavenward together.

I may indeed have to say to you, "Hold your distance."
"Stay in your own place"
I may have to bind you.
But I can create the message,
the reality even,
that will make you realize
there is nothing for you here,
nothing that can make you feel at home.

Perhaps you are open to change,
to mutation, to transformation.
Perhaps you could become my ally,
to the purpose of a greater good.
And even if you take over and run riot,
multiplying and destroying the flesh-body,
you cannot destroy me.
In yourself you are power without love,
and love will triumph over mere power.
Love can take you and calm you and transform you.

Everything will serve the purposes of love,
even that which as yet has no meaning,
and however much pain there may be on the way.
I may become grotesque and faded as flesh-body,
but whenever I live and act
with courage, faith, truth, and compassion,
something else is taking shape,
a more complex, subtle, soul-body,
as yet invisible,
vibrating, as it were, at such a wavelength,
that it cannot be perceived by earthly senses,
which will emerge fully only when I die...

IX. WEAKNESS AND COMPASSION

WE are all incredibly fragile and vulnerable.
Each of us has a lost child within.
Look into the eyes of the suffering man or woman,
and see the grief, pleading, fear, courage, anger.
How can you not show compassion?
If you are without sin – sexual or otherwise –
then throw the stones.
Otherwise, give to each and all the respect
owed to them simply because they are human.

Dear God,
may this disease bring forth in us a new tenderness,
especially for the ones we are tempted to despise.

Being weak is not the end of our influence.
We may indeed be a weak spot, a powerless place,
but this may become the exact point
through which mercy can flow into our lives
and into the lives of those with whom we have to do.
If others sense that we know in depth
the trials of suffering and dying,
they will beat a path to our door,
and will find for themselves some measure of healing.
We shall indeed be 'priests',
living at the centre of sacrifice,
that utter giving
upon which the world depends for everything.

X. SEARCHING FOR A NEW CLARITY

THERE is another side to a new disease
which is not publicly obvious or glamorous,
and which involves a humble sitting before the facts:
the painstaking, laborious, detailed search for a cure.
The work is hidden drudgery and tedium,
and is mostly unsung.
But a discovery might mean that we shall have found a way
to cure the common cold and 'flu...
Thank God for the gift of skills
to probe the mysteries of the universe...
Pray for those whose work is hidden and boring...

Another part of a total healing
is the facing of truths,
and the sharing of information,
about matters previously hidden by fear and taboo.
There is an insistent pressure now to de-mystify sex.
Honesty and clarity have an opportunity to surface
where there has been too much denial and ignorance.

There is a new clarity too about the questions
we need to ask about the best ways of becoming whole
through our relationships:

> How can the strength of the erotic
> nourish healing and growth in two people?

>> What kinds of touch will best heal,
>> will best help to make love,
>> between these two people now?

> What forms of relationships will best enable
> delight, pleasure, enjoyment?

How can the sexual be integrated into a relationship,
so as to give that relationship depth and meaning?

>> Why do we draw close,
>> how do we draw close,
>> and with what result?

>> Is not the end celebration,
>> which has no end?

XI. TOWARDS HEALING SEXUAL WOUNDS

SOME thoughts towards the healing of sexual wounds,
and towards freedom from compulsive behaviour:

Remember the occasion of your wounding,
how you were hurt by another or by yourself.
Remember the person who used you, abused you,
or the person you yourself used.

Remember when sexual desire took you over
and you became less than human,
when force blotted out care.
Remember when you were overpowered by another's desire.

Let your feelings rise – grief, anger, fear,
and express them with noise and movement.
Ask somebody to be with you as you do this,
a person who will simply receive you
and your feelings together, without comment.

Lay quietly on one side the spirit of possessiveness,
of the unmet ancient needs for comfort,
for recognition, for affirmation.
Lay aside too the spirit of violence,
the desire for revenge.
Turn to self-acceptance, a sense of inner worth,
a willingness to stand and to be and to affirm.

Let thoughts drop into the heart,
Let desires rise through the heart.
Let love spread through the heart.

Cherish your flesh-body.

Breathe into your loneliness and go deep,
and then move gently into what you choose to do next.

Be thankful for athletic beauty,
(even if the psalmist said
that God takes no delight in any man's legs).

Laugh at yourself long and out loud.

All these will never be enough
to assuage all the pain.
Simply bear whatever pain that will not shift.
There may be no meaning yet.

XII. LETTING GO IN SEX AND IN DEATH

BECAUSE of the letting go of self
that can occur at the height of orgasm,
there is a hint of death in sexual intercourse.
Because of a new sexually transmittable virus,
with the potential for disfigurement and death,
that hint is now shouting.
Physically and psychologically,
AIDS is omnipresent where sex is concerned.
It nudges us to come to terms with death.
It reminds us that there are limits
to the satisfactions of making love sexually.
Within it there always seems to be the desire for more –
in terms both of repetition
and of deeper and more lasting union.
Sex never yields all that it promises.
The challenge is to be glad for what it does yield
and also to acknowledge its limitations,
and so to live in the tension,
accepting that all our unions are transient.

And the opportunity is given us to get to know
"the root and depth in thee
from whence all thy faculties come forth
as lines from a centre,
or as branches from the body of a tree.
This depth is called the centre, the fund,
or bottom of the soul." (3)

"Such is the deep Christ-Self at the core of us,
the realm of abundant life,
the indestructible deep centre that never gives way,
the small seed which will become the great tree,
the leaven transforming the lump, the eye of the soul,
the ground of being, the heart, the transcendent self,
the extreme point at which God touches us." (4)

XIII. TOUCHING

DISHEVELLED, slouching, he approached her.
He asked for tenpence towards a cup of tea.
She was a nun: perhaps he thought she'd be an easy touch.
She hadn't the money,
but spontaneously she put her hand on his shoulder.
He wept.
No one had touched him for years...

Fear makes us draw back.
Love expels fear and impels us towards the other.
Jesus touched the unclean,
the ones who were believed to contaminate, to pollute.
He touched the leper, the menstruating woman,
the supposed corpse of a child.

Touch can affirm,
reassure, heal,
release creativity.

Sex is the touch of death – and of life.
Through this touch
a woman may die in childbirth;
a child in the womb may be born premature and die;
an infection may pass from one to another;
a compulsive action may be repeated
and a gentler self die a little;
self-centredness may die and love may flourish;
there is the hint of the next generation
who will soon displace us.

Matter shared, fluid exchanged –
through such means we draw close spiritually.
There is no such thing as the purity of the race:
without mingling there is sterility.

So through touch, through matter, through mingling,
we are invited to draw close in communion...

Let us draw near, let us draw very close,
in faith, in deep but trembling trust,
and take into ourselves this bread and wine,
this body, this blood, this intimate presence,
of Yeshua, our Lover and our God.

Beloved, we draw near to be loved by you,
in and through this matter of your creation,
this material stuff of bread and body,
this fluid of wine and blood,
that your desire for us and ours for you
may be blended in deep joy and ecstasy,
that we may be enriched and doubly blessed.

We draw near to receive this offering of yourself,
your intimate, vulnerable, and naked body,
imparted to us, incorporated in us,
that we may dwell and love and create,
we in you and you in us.

(1) Written by the author for an evening of meditation in support of The
    Parsonage, the Episcopal Church's outreach to the gay community in San
    Francisco, November 1986.
(2) From a collection of meditations published by the Sisters of the Love of
    God, Fairacres, Oxford, and used with permission.
(3) William Law.
(4) Evelyn Underhill.

6
Praying for healing – locating the prayer

GOD promises to make whole:
God is faithful.

God wants us to grow to maturity
and this need not be hindered if illness persists.

God seeks our willing co-operation,
in trust and obedience,
when we know what to do and can do it,
and also when we do not know what is happening,
and can do nothing but let be and let go.

God's love is already at work within us,
for we are being created and re-created in God's image,
however marred and distorted it may be.

With our willingness,
by stillness or skill,
by means known or means not understood,
God is present in human lives
willing and working for our healing.

Nothing can separate us from the loving presence of God.

The Love of God strives to transform all evil and pain.

39

There is prayer in the rage of someone in great pain
and in the person who sits silently with another in pain.

There is prayer in urgent asking,
in heartfelt crying and hammering at heaven's door,
expectant of a response.

There is prayer in offering pain
in patience and perseverance,
gently pressing into the grain of that pain,
yielding to its truth.

There is prayer in bearing one another's burdens.

An answer to prayer may be given,
even if it is not exactly what we prayed for.

Pray for courage to face
whatever is blocking God's healing work
in you, in us, in the world.

God's final purposes are known
only *through* the grave and gate of death.

The goal of healing is the glorification of the universe.

Pray for grace, truth, goodness, love, beauty, peace.
Pray for Christlikeness, even in grotesque disfigurement.
The disfigured *will* be transfigured.

The ministry of healing
is a gift to the whole people of God.
Some may have particular gifts to offer,
but they are to be enjoyed for the good of the community
as well as that of the individual.
No gift is to be exercised
in a quirky, bizarre, or individualistic way.

Ask this:
Are we a body of people
among whom those who are dis-eased will find healing,
or is our common life in such disarray
that we shall block and hinder that healing?

7
Praying for healing –
approaching the prayer

I. WHO DOES WHAT WHERE?

WHAT follows is meant as a resource for individual and corporate prayer for healing. It is not meant to be followed slavishly. There is a certain logic to the sequence of sections, but nothing fixed and final about it. The trouble with the printed word is that it lends an excess of authority to what is written, simply by reason of the fact that it is printed. It is important that we are on the inside of words of prayer, and whoever is using this selection should take responsibility and choose what is helpful, adapt where necessary, and not feel guilty at leaving something out.

In some of the prayers and biddings it is assumed that one person is addressing another or the whole company. '1' may, in different circumstances, be minister, priest, leader, fellow pilgrim(s), and '2' may be penitent, congregation, fellow pilgrim(s). Many groups and congregations will find it typically (but not necessarily universally) appropriate for '1' to be the person(s) recognized as representing, enabling, and embodying that group, congregation, or wider church.

However, in informal settings it may be appropriate to substitute 'we' for 'I' and 'you'. This could be important when praying with those who are stigmatized and blamed for their illness. It is not the case that 'I who am healthy will now pray for you who are ill', but that we are all praying together in our shared pain and suffering.

It is also worth asking if a laying on of hands or anointing with oil might be mutual. If a person is not too ill, he or she could lay hands on or anoint those who have come to minister. It may seem a strange reversal, but the gifts of the weak and the last gifts of the dying may be a deep healing grace to those who at the time are the more obviously strong.

Prayer for healing can clearly take place anywhere, and in some instances will be dictated by the condition of the one who is ill. If the ministry is to one individual, a certain privacy, even if indicated only by curtains drawn round a bed in a hospital ward, will be appropriate. Or the praying may take place in the privacy of a person's home or the semi-privacy of a place of 'hospital-ity', a hospice or a nursing 'home'. In such locations the architecture will be consonant with the activity.

Is this the case with churches? Gothic churches reflect a hierarchical understanding of community life with the king or emperor at its head. But how many of us today experience the king as the healer? Nonconformist chapels reflect a theology of judgment, modelled on the lawcourt. But how many of us experience the judge as the wise discerner of justice and the one who can enable broken relationships to be healed?

These are metaphors which are hard to claim by the individual who seeks a measure of healing through sacramental ritual in church. And they are metaphors which once connected with the social order, with the life of the community. This book hardly touches on the kind of ritual which might be devised which seeks and symbolizes the healing of the community's wounds. We just do not have an architecture or a symbolism that can link religious faith with the everyday corporate life of village, town, or city. The most we can perhaps hope for is large empty spaces and imaginative experiments.

II. THANKING AND CONFESSING

BECAUSE the Church has concentrated the attention more on confessing sins than on gratitude for gifts given, the prayers in this section seek to redress the balance. They provide an opportunity for *specific* thanksgivings as well as for confessing specific failures to love. Gratitude for gifts given to us, and gratitude expressed by another for who we are and what we have done, is more likely than cool criticism or hostile accusation to inspire us to face more difficult truths about ourselves and to determine upon change.

Both gratitude and penitence, individual and corporate, are integral parts of the healing process, for they release us from bitterness and from the gnawing and nibbling of guilt and memories. Both hinder our loving.

Although there is no simple and direct causal link between sin and suffering (see chapter 5), they do overlap as part of the world's at-wrong-ness, and we grow in grace only by taking responsibility for our contribution to the dis-ease.

The reconciliation that comes through confession and forgiveness leads directly, in the service of Holy Communion, to the gifts of Peace and Celebration: the Sharing of the Peace and the Eucharistic Prayer.

At the moment of absolution, marked in the text by the word 'Silence', it may be appropriate for the one who has been receiving the confession to place a hand on the neck of the other – that most important 'connecting' part of the body. This kind of sacramental reassurance at one of the places where we feel most vulnerable can help to anchor and earth the exchange of love and through it give greater spiritual depth to that exchange.

III. SPEAKING WITH TONGUES

'SPEAKING with tongues', widespread among peoples of different faiths and of none, seems to be one of the God-given mechanisms of release from emotional burdens and a means of reassurance of worth for those who have been browbeaten by the powerful who have the gift of persuasive speech. Where people are not afraid of this phenomenon, and there is an atmosphere of quiet openness and steady leadership, speaking with tongues can be a healing grace both for an individual and for a congregation who let themselves relax into what can often sound like a gently murmuring stream. The only reason there is no reference to this in the next chapter is that there can be no script!

Walter Hollenweger, a Swiss Pentecostalist minister and later a professor of mission, alerts us to the healing purpose of speaking with tongues, and in the enclosing paragraphs John V. Taylor gives this judicious summary, written some years ago in a newsletter of the Church Missionary Society.

"Whether for the individual who is too exhausted to pray or at a loss for words, or the group that is much despised by the verbalizers and dare not be articulate, speaking in tongues is profoundly therapeutic... Need is met. Unconscious tensions are released. Loneliness is appeased. Sickness is healed. Uncertainties about the future are resolved. Inarticulate weakness finds expression.

" 'Whether it exists among the agricultural workers of Chile, the Indians of Argentina, the proletariat of North America, the masses of African cities, the gypsies of France, the members of Swedish trades unions, or the poor in Britain, the function of the Pentecostal movement is to restore the power of speech, and to heal them from the terror of the loss of speech...'

"All the Spirit's gifts are wonderful, all are marked by a certain spontaneity; but none is meant to be weird. They are incalculable, they are corporate. Christian healing is essentially the gift, not of particularly endowed individuals, but of the Spirit-filled community.'

IV. LOOSENING, SEPARATING, GREETING

A MINISTRY of deliverance can be of help to those who, in imagination or in form of belief, can pray and be prayed for in such terms. The process is one of being loosened from deep-rooted compulsions, for example, or from the incessant presence of a person, living or departed, from whom we should now be separated. The prayer can focus on God some of the painstaking uncovering of the past that emerges in the healing work of counselling and therapy.

V. THE LAYING ON OF HANDS

MANY are the informal moments of healing where one person lays hands on another. For hands can soothe and comfort. They can touch a person wracked with pain in such a way as to bring relief. They can massage away tensions in the muscles and help to harmonize the energies of the body. They can radiate a healing warmth.

There are some who have a specific ability, also a gift to be enjoyed and used, of healing through their hands. They may talk of different wavelengths of energy, experiencing that which in our culture we barely understand.

So much of the healing work of hands goes on in ordinary or professional contexts apart from occasions of informal blessing and more formal ritual. Symbolically too, hands are laid on others at special, once-for-all, rites of passage, witnessed and supported by the community. Examples are the moments of entering one's adult inheritance of faith and ministry at Confirmation and of entering the gift of the ministry of leadership at Ordination. The laying on of hands, then, can be a sacramental means of our being built up together in the love and service of God.

The laying on of hands for healing can also happen informally and in private, but in church or chapel it is more likely to focus our corporate prayer and concern. When hands are laid on a person in church it is usually done by those who represent and lead the local Christian community, together with those for whom the work of healing is their special care. Like all such acts it is done on behalf of everyone, not instead of them. In a corporate act of worship we demonstrate publicly that healing is one of the major concerns of Christian practice. The public event focuses that concern, and offers *all* the work of healing, wherever it occurs, to God for blessing.

Further, since this is the work of the whole community, and since we are bound up so closely with one another in our disease and healing, I think there is something to be said for the old custom of receiving the laying on of hands on behalf of someone you know, who, for example, may be ill in hospital miles away.

And I would again emphasise that there is no reason at all why *anyone* should not lay hands on any other who wishes it, in a gesture, a small sacrament, of prayer and support, of healing and blessing. Indeed the mutuality of giving and receiving can be particularly healing, not least if the group itself has come through a time of stress and conflict. The only concern should be that any gift of healing exercised in a one-to-one way should be done in a context of continuing friendship or pastoral care.

VI. ANOINTING WITH OIL

As with hands, so with oil and ointment: we can distinguish between an informal use, in private, one to one, to ease inflamed joints or to give a sense of warmth and well-being, perhaps with the use of different aromatic oils, and the very formal special use as part of a once-for-all ritual, the anointing of monarch or bishop for a particularly burdensome and responsible commission.

There may also be an anointing at Baptism and Confirmation, as part of that focusing of our being bathed and cleansed by God and our being sealed, as oil 'seals' water, by the Holy Spirit.

Then there is the anointing with oil for healing, again either publicly or privately. But what distinguishes its purpose from that of the laying on of hands?

Some disease does not go away. It would be cruel to raise a person's expectations that by a laying on of hands brain damage might suddenly be overcome or years of emotional pain might suddenly evaporate as though they had never been. If severe damage has been done to an infant, physical or emotional, the road to deep healing takes time and is costly. It will be a way of the cross, a royal road maybe, but rough. Moreover, at some time in our lives we have to begin to learn that the goal is not cure but Christlikeness. There were no legions of angels rescuing Jesus from pain and dying. He endured, and at great cost.

We read in the Gospels of a woman of no great reputation anointing Jesus with expensive ointment some days before this death. He received this gesture as a kind of consecrating of the way he was to go, the way of the cross, of dying, and of burial. No one could share it with him, no one could share the moment of his dying. And no one can share ours. But those around us, looking on, can at least be there for us, supporting and blessing and caring.

Intractable illness and this story of the anointing of Jesus for burial may give us a clue to the purpose of anointing with oil. Oil of course was a common medicine in the time of Jesus, and anointing was a frequent practice in the life of the early Church. It is mentioned in the Letter of James, 5.14. Centuries later Bede of Jarrow wrote of the way in which oil that had been blessed in church was taken home by the people, where they administered anointing to one another. By the twelfth century, however, it had become 'extreme unction', a ministry of anointing by the priest alone, and only at the point of death.

This may be too narrow a way of understanding anointing, but the instinct may have been a sure one that linked it with some profound, life-changing event, some crisis that a person has to face alone.

Death is one obvious example. There does come the time when we have to recognize that death is imminent: there is nothing more in this world's terms that can be done, save an appropriate leave-taking and blessing.

But there are other critical times. A person may have to face a dark and lonely inner journey in order to understand and transform some compulsive pattern of behaviour or to be reconciled with the frightened, hurt, lonely child within who has been crying silently in the night for years. Sexual abuse can be one such event that needs to be recalled in order to be healed, and some suggestions are given in Appendix B for an anointing in such circumstances.

Or we may ask for anointing that we may bear the lonely burden of a ministry of constant care for a schizophrenic son or a chronically ill mother or a daughter who cannot see or hear.

We cannot follow one another into these places. There are depths which even the wisest cannot plumb. When someone we love is so suffering, we are like the disciples of Jesus in the Garden of Gethsemane. We cannot go with him in his unique struggle. The most we can do is to watch and pray. "I will be here for you, on the edge, and I may even fall asleep, but I will be here."

The anointing with oil can then be understood as a consecration on the way of one's deepest truth, going through a Gethsemane alone. To be anointed is to seek the courage to lay oneself open completely to the love and will of God, even if it involves a cup that you would choose not to drink.

Faith may strengthen us in such circumstances, trust in the reliability and grace of God, faith that we shall touch no ground where Christ has not been. We have to go our own way of the cross, but the depths of pain and loss have been sounded for us. And in the midst of it all we may sense Christ's sustaining presence. So the oil of anointing becomes the oil of gladness and rejoicing. Lamps are lit in the darkest of places, in the deepest dungeons of all, where maybe even Satan yearns to become again an angel of light.

And the one who is anointed may be the one to anoint us in our turn. The sufferer may heal us, a thought which hardly ever crosses our minds in the days of our strength. The trust and openness of the mentally handicapped may bring a grieving widow out of her isolation, and together they may know something of the peace which passes understanding.

Little more can be said. We are on holy ground. We have reached the point in our praying where we fall silent before a great mystery, that of suffering *redeemed,* not by being taken away, not by magic, but by going through it until it yields to joy.

8
Praying for healing –
entering the prayer

I. PREPARING AND REFLECTING

A TIME to align oneself to the Love of God,
within and beyond,
to become aware of those around who are also praying...

A time to relax and become still...

Stretch... Shake... Settle...

Sit with back straight up and down
and with both feet on the ground...

Breathe out gently and a long way,
and then simply let the air in...

Relax into any aches and pains...

No strain... Relax... Let be...

Bring a word to mind such as
Peace, Healing, Spirit...

Bring a picture to mind such as
Running water, Wide ocean, Caring hands...

Abide in the Presence...

Living, loving God, our Father and Mother,
the Source of life and health, of strength and of peace,
show us the Way, the Truth, and the Life;
take from us all that hinders the flow of your Spirit;
with hands of compassion wash away our sin and fear,
our resentment and hardness of heart;
enable us to become centred and still,
aware of your Presence, here, now,
to heal, to redeem, to transform...
We pray in the Spirit of Jesus Christ our Healing Saviour.

II. THANKING AND CONFESSING

a. For an individual

1   THE Spirit of the Living God be with you.
2   The Peace of Christ dwell in your heart.

1 & 2   From the deep places of my soul
           I praise you, O God:
           I lift up my heart
           and glorify your holy name.
           How can I forget
           all your goodness towards me?
           You forgive all my sin,
           you heal all my weakness,
           you rescue me from the brink of disaster,
           you crown me with mercy and compassion.
           You are full of forgiveness and grace,
           endlessly patient, faithful in love.
           As vast as the heavens are
           in comparison with the earth,
           so great is your love
           towards those who trust you.

           Holy God,
           Creator and Sustainer of the world,
           holy and utterly loving,
           we give you thanks and praise.

2   Eternal God, Giver of all good gifts,
           I your friend and servant
           now give you humble and hearty thanks
           for all your goodness and loving kindness
           to me and to all the world.
           I bless you for my creation, preservation,
           and all the blessings of this life.

           Especially I thank you for . . .

Above all I thank you for your great love
in the redeeming of the world
by our Saviour Jesus Christ,
for the means of grace
and for the hope of glory.

And I ask of you,
give me that due sense of all your mercies,
that my heart may be unreservedly thankful,
and that I show forth your praise,
not only with my lips but in my life,
by giving up myself to your service,
and by walking before you
in holiness and righteousness all my days;

through Jesus Christ my Redeemer,
to whom with you and the Holy Spirit
be all honour and glory,
now and for ever. Amen.

1   For God's gift of you to us,
for all that you are and all that you give,
I too thank and praise our faithful Creator.

1 & 2   Enfold me in your love, dear God,
yet pierce my heart with your mercy.
In the cascading of your compassion
scour away all that offends.
Wash me thoroughly from my wickedness,
and cleanse me from my sin.
My failures weigh heavy on my heart,
my sin confronts me at the turning of the road.
Against you alone have I sinned, my Beloved,
doing what is evil and causing more harm.
In the eyes of my victims your judgment is clear:
there is nothing I can claim in your presence.
I was formed in the midst of a world gone wrong:
from the moment of my conceiving
I breathed my ancestors' sin.

The truths of my sin are hidden
so deep, so secretly:
bring the light of your wisdom
to the depths of my heart.

Holy God,
holy in refining and mercy,
holy and utterly loving,
have mercy upon us.

2   The sacrifice you ask is a troubled spirit:
it is my pride that must yield to you, my God.
My broken and contrite heart I bring,
so foolish, self-centred, and vain –
and yet it is all that I have.
Even this gift you will not despise.
For I hear again that you yearn for me,
with a love I can barely imagine.

My friend in God, pray for me, a sinner.

1   May the piercing light of Christ
illuminate your heart and mind,
that you may remember in truth
all your sins and God's unfailing mercy.
For we also remember, dear God,
how much you love us and all the world;
you have given yourself to us in Jesus Christ,
that we might not perish
but have abundant and eternal life.

2   My beloved and faithful Creator,
you formed me from the dust in your image,
and you redeemed me from sin and death
through the living, dying, and rising
of the One who is your very Word made flesh.
Through baptism you accepted me, cleansed me,
and gave me new life.
You called me to your service and friendship.

But I have wounded your love
and marred your image.
I have wandered far in a land that is waste.
Especially do I confess to you, dear God,
and to my sisters and brothers, your people...

[*This is the place for confessing particular sins.*]

Therefore, dear God, from these sins
and from those I cannot now remember,
I turn to you in sorrow, in repentance,
and in trust.

Cast me not away from your presence,
and take not your Holy Spirit from me.
Give me the comfort of your help again,
and strengthen me with courage and hope.
Receive me in your mercy
and restore me to the company of your people.

1   True love, divine love, is sure and steady,
absorbing your hurt, never deflected by it,
accepting tragedy and redeeming it,
involved with you, closer to you than breathing,
exposed and vulnerable to everything you do,
working within you the pattern of that love.

True love, divine love,
gladly receives the truths of your heart,
runs with delight to embrace you,
favours you at the banquet of joy.

Jesus embodied that love,
and called us to embody it too.
To those who promised
to weave its pattern
the Spirit was given that we might choose
to forgive or withhold forgiveness,
to enable or to hinder the forgiveness of God.

In the name and in the Spirit of Jesus,
aware of that gift of forgiveness,
and seeking to embody the Gospel
of unconditional love,
with the voice of Christ
resonating deep within me,
and on behalf of all the people
who follow the Way, then and now,
I... forgive... you...

[*Silence*]

Be assured that you are forgiven,
forgiven by Christ,
forgiven by your fellow-pilgrims,
released from all that hurts you.

2   Amen. Thanks be to God.

1   Do you gladly give yourself again to Christ,
to follow the narrow way that leads to life,
and to keep your eyes fixed on Christ,
who is the goal and the glory?

2   I do.

1   Will you, in the strength of God's forgiveness,
seek to be reconciled with those
who have sinned against you,
and where that is not now possible,
will you keep open a forgiving heart and will?

2   I will.

1   Abide in peace.
God has put away all your sins.
You are restored to the people of God.
Rejoice and be glad.

2   Alleluia. Thanks be to God.

b. For the whole body

1 THE Spirit of the Living God be with you.

2 The Peace of Christ dwell in your heart.

1 & 2 From the deep places of our souls
we praise you, O God:
we lift up our hearts
and glorify your holy name.
How can we forget
all your goodness towards us?
You forgive all our sin,
you heal all our weakness,
you rescue us from the brink of disaster,
you crown us with mercy and compassion.
You are full of forgiveness and grace,
endlessly patient, faithful in love.
As vast at the heavens are
in comparison with the earth,
so great is your love
towards those who trust you.

Holy God,
Creator and Sustainer of the world,
holy and utterly loving,
we give you thanks and praise.

1 Let us go deep into silence,
in gratitude and trust...

[*A time of silence*]

1 & 2 Eternal God, Giver of all good gifts,
we your friends and servants
now give you humble and hearty thanks
for all your goodness and loving kindness
to us and to all the world.
We bless you for our creation, preservation,
and all the blessings of this life.

1 Especially we thank you for...

[*The particular thanksgivings of the community*]

1 & 2   Above all we thank you for your great love
in the redeeming of the world
by our Saviour Jesus Christ,
for the means of grace
and for the hope of glory.

And we ask of you,
give us that due sense of all your mercies,
that our hearts may be unreservedly thankful,
and that we show forth your praise,
not only with our lips but with our lives,
by giving up ourselves to your service,
and by walking before you
in holiness and righteousness all our days;

through Jesus Christ our Redeemer,
to whom with you and the Holy Spirit,
be all honour and glory,
now and for ever. Amen.

1 & 2   Enfold us in your love, dear God,
yet pierce our hearts with your mercy.
In the cascading of your compassion
scour away all that offends.
Wash us thoroughly from our wickedness,
and cleanse us from our sin.
Our failures weigh heavy on our hearts,
our sin confronts us at the turning of the road.
Against you alone have we sinned,
doing what is evil and causing more harm.
In the eyes of our victims
your judgment is clear:
there is nothing we can claim
in your presence.
We were formed in the midst
of a world gone wrong:
from the moment of our conceiving
we breathed our ancestors' sin.

The truths of our sin are hidden
so deep, so secretly:
bring the light of your wisdom
to the depths of our hearts.

Holy God,
holy in refining and mercy,
holy and utterly loving,
have mercy upon us.

The sacrifice you ask is a troubled spirit:
it is our pride that must yield to you, O God.
Our broken and contrite hearts we bring,
so foolish, self-centred, and vain –
and yet it is all that we have.
Even this gift you will not despise.
For we hear again that you yearn for us,
with a love we can barely imagine.

1   May the piercing light of Christ
illuminate our hearts and minds,
that we may remember in truth
all our sins and God's unfailing mercy.
For we also remember, dear God,
how much you love us and all the world;
you have given yourself to us in Jesus Christ,
that we might not perish
but have abundant life.

1 & 2   Beloved and faithful Creator,
you formed us from the dust in your image,
and you redeemed us from sin and death
through the living, dying, and rising
of the One who is your very Word made flesh.
Through baptism you accepted us, cleansed us,
and gave us new life.
You called us to your service and friendship.
But we have wounded your love
and marred your image.
We have wandered far in a land that is waste.

1   Especially do we confess to you, dear God,
           and to our brothers and sisters, your people...

           [*This is the place for the naming of the
           particular sin and sins of the body.*]

1 & 2   Therefore, dear God, from these sins
           and from those we cannot now remember,
           we turn to you in sorrow, in repentance,
           and in trust.

           Cast us not away from your presence,
           and take not your Holy Spirit from us.
           Give us the comfort of your help again,
           and strengthen us with courage and hope.
           Receive us in your mercy
           and restore us to the company of your people.

1   True love, divine love, is sure and steady,
           absorbing our hurt, never deflected by it,
           accepting tragedy and redeeming it,
           involved with us, closer to us than breathing,
           exposed and vulnerable to everything we do,
           working among us the pattern of that love.

           True love, divine love,
           gladly receives the truths of our heart,
           runs with delight to embrace us,
           favours us at the banquet of joy.

           Jesus embodied that love,
           and called us to embody it too.
           To those who promised
           to weave its pattern
           the Spirit was given that we might choose
           to forgive or withhold forgiveness,
           to enable or to hinder the forgiveness of God.

In the name and in the Spirit of Jesus,
aware of that gift of forgiveness,
and seeking to embody the Gospel
of unconditional love,
with the voice of Christ
resonating deep within us,
let us say, each to all,

1 & 2   I... forgive... you...,

[*Silence*]

1   and let us hear the word of Christ,
to us the Body of Christ,
I... forgive... you...

[*Silence*]

Be assured that we are forgiven,
forgiven by Christ,
forgiven by our fellow-pilgrims,
released from all that hurts us.

2   Amen. Thanks be to God.

1   Let us live together in the forgiveness of God,
and greet one another in peace.

III. PRAYING FOR OTHERS

Response: Healing Spirit, set us free.

> FROM wearisome pain...
> From the sharp sword of agony...
> From burdens too great to bear in love for others...
> From guilt and regret about times past...
> From fearful memories and fear for the future...
> From the grip of compulsions...
> From pride, greed, and bitterness...
> From illusion, lying, and pretence...
> From the depths of despair...

Response: Spirit of God, heal us.

Through the ministry of those who serve the public health...
Through the ministry of those who work in preventive
   medicine and health education...
Through the ministry of prophets who show the powers of
   industry and commerce their contribution to disease...
Through the ministry of those who seek to guard the health of
   air and soil and oceans...
Through the ministry of those who administer the health
   service and who make financial decisions on our behalf...
Through the ministry of those who care in hospital, home,
   and hospice...
Through the ministry of listening and of presence...
Through the bearing of one another's burdens...
Through the ministry of counselling and therapy...
Through the ministry of prayer and sacrament...
Through our expectant hearts and open minds...
Through the bringing of our wills into harmony with your
   loving purpose...
Through our joy in being the friends of God...
In the hour of our dying...
In the transfiguring of evil and pain...

The creation will be set free from bondage to decay,
and obtain the glorious liberty of the children of God.

IV. PRAYING IN CHRIST

ETERNAL Spirit,
Life-giver, Pain-bearer, Love-maker,
Source of all that is and that shall be,
Father and Mother of us all,
Loving God, in whom is heaven:

The Hallowing of your Name
echo through the universe;
The Way of your Justice
be followed by the peoples of the world;
Your Heavenly Will
be done by all created beings;
Your Commonwealth of Peace and Freedom
sustain our hope and come on earth.

With the bread we need for today,
feed us.
In the hurts we absorb from one another,
forgive us.
In times of temptation and test,
strengthen us.
From trials too great to endure,
spare us.
From the grip of all that is evil,
free us.

For you reign in the glory
of the power that is love,
now and for ever. Amen.

V. LOOSENING, SEPARATING, GREETING

PEOPLE of God,
within us and among us and through the world,
there are many powers of dis-ease
which hold us in their grip.
They trouble us, distract us, wound us.
They go by many names:
greed, pride, loneliness;
fear, rage, grief;
pain, death, evil...
some known in the secret places of our hearts,
some as yet unknown to us,
some greater in strength
than any one of us can bear alone...

Let us be silent awhile
and pray in the name of God,
Liberator, Redeemer, Healer,
revealed to us in Jesus of Nazareth...

[*A period of silence*]

May we seek to understand and withstand these powers,
to know their name and nature,
that they may cease their hold on us,
and be transformed by the power of that Love
that is deeper than the deepest pain,
that we may be freed to be the friends of God.

A prayer focusing on the needs of a particular person

In the name of Jesus Christ,
come out of darkness into light, [N].*
Help us to understand and withstand you,
that we may know your name and nature,
that you may wound us no more,
that you may yield your energy
in the service of God.

* It may be appropriate to name what is troubling
a person, for example, a spirit of revenge.

And where through lack of prayer or fasting,
through weak will or fainthearted love,
through the mysteries of the unresolved,
through fear of your destructive power,
we cannot yet be reconciled,
leave us be,
depart to the place where, one day,
we shall all face the refining flame
of the judging, healing, loving God.

VI. LAYING ON OF HANDS

A prayer of preparation

BLESSED are you, eternal God,
Source of all healing,
for you have given us the means
by which you make your creatures whole,
our presence and our skills,
our understanding of your laws
and our humility before the unknown,
our words and our hands,
medicines that soothe and cure,
machines that aid our work.

We give ourselves to you:
empty us of all that hinders the flow
of your healing Spirit;
take our hands and our lives
that we may live in your image
and reflect your glory.

Bidding to all

> In the name of God,
> who is great and good and love,
> in the name of God,
> giving life, bearing pain, making whole:
>
> by the laying on of these (our) hands
> may the healing Spirit bless and support us/you,
> for we/you are dearly loved;
>
> by the laying on of these (our) hands
> may the healing Spirit flow freely
> in us/you and through us/you,
> the power that is waiting to be set free among us,
> that seeks our will and consent and trust;
>
> by the laying on of these (our) hands
> may the healing Spirit confirm us in our faith,
> making us strong together as one Body
> in the service and friendship of Christ.

To each who receives the laying on of hands

> N, through the laying on of these hands
> and through our prayer,
> receive the gift of the healing Spirit of God.

or

> N, may the Holy Spirit,
> the Giver of all life and healing,
> fill you with Light and Love,
> and make you whole;
> through Jesus Christ our Saviour.

VII. ANOINTING

Blessing of the oil

ETERNAL and loving God,
bless this oil
and bless those who receive its anointing in trust,
that it may be to them
an eternal medicine,
a spiritual remedy,
an inward consecration,
to their strengthening, healing, and joy;
through Jesus Christ our Saviour.

Bidding to all

In the name of God,
who is great and good and love,
in the name of God,
giving life, bearing pain, making whole:

by this oil
may we/you be warmed and soothed:
may the healing Spirit
penetrate the cells and fibres of our/your being,
that we/you may become whole,
giving thanks to God always and in all places,
and being ready to venture further on the way of faith;

by this oil
may we/you renew the consecration of our/your life
to the truth and service of God,
being not afraid to encounter God alone,
nor of dying in order to live,
nor of bearing the burdens of others
with whom we/you have do to;

know this oil
as a sign of gladness and rejoicing,
of lamps lit and of feasting,
of mirth and of joy.

To each who receives anointing

> N, through faith in the power and the will
> of our Saviour Jesus Christ
> to make you whole and holy,
> to consecrate you with joy
> for ever deeper service and friendship,
> to give you courage
> to go through the narrow gates of your journey,
> I anoint you with oil
> in the name of God, ·
> who gives you life,
> bears your pain,
> and makes you whole.
> Amen.

VIII. TRUSTING

A prayer in the Celtic tradition

> SPIRIT of God be
> within me to strengthen me,
> beyond me to draw me,
> over me to shelter me,
> beneath me to support me,
> before me to guide me,
> behind me to steady me,
> round about me to secure me.

A prayer based on part of the Letter to the Ephesians

> According to the riches of God's glory,
> may we be strengthened with might
> through the Spirit in our inner being,
> and may Christ dwell in our hearts through faith,
> that being rooted and grounded in love,
> we may have power to comprehend with all the saints
> what is the breath and length and height and depth,
> and to know the love of Christ which passes knowledge,
> that we may be filled with all the fulness of God.

A prayer based on one by Charles de Foucauld

Abba, I abandon myself into your hands...
In your love for me do as you will...
Whatever that may prove to be I am thankful...
I am ready for all, I accept all...
Let only your will be done in me,
    as in all your creatures,
    and I will ask nothing else...
Into your hands I commend my whole being...
I give myself to you with the love of my heart...
For I love you, my God, and so I need to give,
    to surrender myself into your hands
    with a trust beyond measure...
For you are my faithful Creator...
May I indeed be your friend...

IX. BLESSING

RECEIVE a blessing
for all that may be required of you,
that love may drive out fear,
that you may be more perfectly
abandoned to the will of God,
that peace and contentment
may reign in your hearts,
and through you may spread
over the face of the earth.

The blessing of God,
Giver of life,
Bearer of pain,
Maker of love,
Creator and Sustainer,
Liberator and Redeemer,
Healer and Sanctifier,
be with you and all whom you love,
both living and departed,
now and for ever. Amen.

X. DYING

1   PEACE be to this house and all who live here.

1 & 2   We confess to God who is all Love,
        Father, Son, and Holy Spirit,
        that we have sinned in thought, word, and deed,
        and in what we have left undone.

1   The God of Love and Mercy
        forgive you and all of us our sins
        and keep us in eternal life. Amen.

1 & 2   Our Father, who art in heaven,
        hallowed be thy name,
        thy kingdom come, thy will be done,
        on earth as it is in heaven.
        Give us this day our daily bread.
        Forgive us our trespasses,
        as we forgive those who trespass against us.
        and lead us not into temptation,
        but deliver us from evil.
        For thine is the kingdom,
        the power, and the glory,
        for ever and ever. Amen.

1   Through our prayer
        and through the laying on of these hands,
        may the Holy Spirit,
        the Giver of all life and healing,
        fill you, N, with light and love,
        and make you whole;
        through Jesus Christ our Saviour. Amen.

        Through this holy anointing
        and through God's great love for you,
        may the Holy Spirit
        move in the depths of your being, N,
        to make you whole and holy;
        and may you be consecrated to God anew,
        now and for eternity. Amen.

N,
go forth upon your journey from this world,
in the name of God the Father who created you,
in the name of Jesus Christ who redeemed you,
in the name of the Holy Spirit who is sanctifying you.
May the angels of God receive you,
and the saints of God welcome you.
May your rest this day be in peace,
and your dwelling the paradise of God.

The Lord bless you and keep you,
the Lord makes his face to shine upon you
    and be gracious to you,
the Lord lift up the light of his countenance upon you,
and give you peace.

And the blessing of the God of Love,
Father, Son, and Holy Spirit,
be with you,
giving you life,
bearing your pain,
making you whole;
may God bring you through the narrow gate
and across the great river,
and may God reconcile us all in joy,
both living and departed,
in the merriment of heaven.

1 & 2 Amen.

APPENDICES

A
Praying through some Psalms

I. A DESPERATE CRY IN TIME OF ILLNESS
A version of Psalm 6

Refrain: I cry out to the Void:
How long, O God, how long?

HIDEOUS afflictions of a turbulent age –
virus, cancer, thrombosis, ulcer –
warheads in the fluids of my being:
I am caught in a world that is twisted,
trapped in its web of corruption,
tempted to blame my ills on to 'them',
tempted to avoid the hatred within.

Hard pressed by anxiety and discord,
carriers of disease, injectors of poison,
overwhelmed by malice and fear,
paralyzed, depressed, we cannot move,
spun in the vortex of death.

Distressed in the very depths of our being,
bones shaking, cells mutating,
we are almost in despair.

In your mercy and grace set us free.
Refine us in the fire of your love.
Our cry is of hope, yet struggling with doubt,
a stammer gasping for breath in the night.

Turn your face to me, save my life;
deliver me in the endurance of love,
ease the burden of guilt and of pain,
let me know the grace of your presence,
now in this life and through the shades of the grave.

Refrain: I cry out to the Void:
How long, O God, how long?

I am weary with my suffering,
every night I flood my bed with tears.
I drench my couch with weeping,
my eyes waste away out of grief,
I grow weak through the weight of oppression.

You that work evil and seek to destroy,
Loosen your grip, away from my presence.
For God has heard the sound of my weeping,
forgives me with delight and lightens my gloom.
The destroyers will be ashamed and sore troubled:
trembling, they will be stripped of their power,
no longer able to harm.

And no, I will not gloat or hate,
in the Love of God I will hold on to you yet.
In the anger and hope of the wrath of our God,
come to the place of repentance and mercy.
And you, silent virus, invisible, malignant,
bound up with my bodily being,
are you an enemy that I can befriend,
or at least contain in a place of your own –
your power to harm taken away,
brought with us to the glory of God?

God of mercy and tenderness, giver of life and conqueror of death, look upon our weakness and pain, and bring us to health and to wholeness, that we may sing a new song to your praise; through Jesus Christ, Redeemer of the powers.

II. THE PAIN OF THE HEART

A version of Psalm 13

Refrain: Warm the pain of my heart
with the lance of your healing.

How long, O God, how long?
You hide your face from me,
you utterly forget me.

How long, O God, how long?
My being is in torment,
my heart is grieved day and night.

How long, O God, how long?
Icy death, dread and despair,
insidious foes, they strengthen their grip.

Dull are my eyes and lifeless,
as I stare at the desolate places.
Give light to my eyes,
stir up my will and my passion,
my trust in your life-giving Spirit.

Fill my heart with compassion and strength,
that I may rejoice in your generous love,
able to strive with my foes,
no longer dead in the depths of my being.

Yes, at the moment of emptiness and dread
you surprise me with joy and deliverance.
I will sing and shout with delight,
for you have overwhelmed me with grace.

O living, loving God, taking to yourself the pains of the world, cherish our
wounded hearts in a tender embrace, and cradle our scars, that we may
witness to your glory; through the Pain-bearer Christ we pray.

III. WHY? WHY? WHY?

A version of Psalm 22

Refrain for Part One: Why, silent God, why?

MY God, my God, why have you forsaken me?
Why are you so far from helping me?
O my God, I howl in the daytime but you do not hear me.
I groan in the watches of the night, but I find no rest.

Yet still you are the holy God whom Israel has long worshipped.
Our ancestors hoped in you, and you rescued them.
They trusted in you, and you delivered them.
They called upon you: you were faithful to your covenant.
They put their trust in you and were not disappointed.

But as for me, I crawl the earth like a worm,
despised by others, an outcast of the people.
All those who see me laugh me to scorn:
they make mouths at me, shaking their heads and saying,
'He threw himself on God for deliverance:
let God rescue him then, if God so delights in him.'

You were my midwife, O God, drawing me out of the womb.
I was weak and unknowing, yet you were my hope –
even as I lay close to the breast,
cast upon you from the days of my birth.
From the womb of my mother to the dread of these days,
you have been my God, never letting me go.

Do not desert me, for trouble is hard at hand,
and there is no one to help me.
Wild beasts close in on me, narrow-eyed, greedy and sleek.
They open their mouths and snarl at me,
like a ravening and roaring lion.

My strength drains away like water, my bones are out of joint;
my heart also in the midst of my body is even like melting wax;

my mouth is dried up like a potsherd, my tongue cleaves to
    my gums;
my hands and my feet are withered, you lay me down in the
    dust of death.

The huntsmen are all about me:
a circle of wicked men hem me in on every side,
their dogs unleashed to tear me apart.
They have pierced my hands and my feet –
I can count all my bones –
they stand staring and gloating over me.
They divide my garments among them,
they cast lots for my clothes.

The tanks of the mighty encircle me,
barbed wire and machine guns surround me.
They have marked my arm with a number,
and never call me by name.
They have stripped me of clothes and of shoes,
and showered me with gas in the chamber of death.

I cry out for morphine but no one hears me.
Pinned down by straitjacket I scream the night through.
I suffocate through panic in the oxygen tent.
Sweating with fear I await news of my doom.

No one comes near with an unmasked face,
no skin touches mine in a gesture of love.
They draw back in terror, speaking only
in whispers behind doors that are sealed.

Be not far from me, O God: you are my helper, hasten to
    my aid.
Deliver my very self from the sword, my life from the falling
    of the axe.
Save me from the mouth of the lion,
poor body that I am, from the horns of the bull.

*Silent God, we bring the cries of our battered hearts, and the cries of those
burdened by illness and bowed down by the weight of oppression. We bring
them so that we may not be silent. Hear us in the name of Jesus, forsaken
on the Cross.*

Refrain for Part Two: Even though you slay me,
yet will I trust you.

I will declare your name to my friends:
in the midst of the congregation I will praise you.
We stand in awe of you and bow down before you,
we glorify and magnify your name.

For you have not shrunk in loathing
from the suffering in their affliction.
You have not hid your face from them,
but when they called to you, you heard them.

My praise is of you in the great congregation,
my vows I will perform in their sight.
We shall praise you with thanksgiving and wonder.
We shall share what we have with the poor:
they shall eat and be satisfied,
a new people, yet to be born.
Those who seek you shall be found by you:
they will be in good heart for ever.

So shall my life be preserved in your sight,
and my children shall worship you:
they shall tell of you to generations yet to come:
to a people yet to be born
they shall declare your righteousness,
that you have brought these things to fulfilment.

So let all the ends of the world remember
and turn again to their God.
Let all the families of the nations worship their Creator.
For all dominion belongs to you,
and you are the ruler of the peoples.

O God of enduring love, whom the clouds obscure, may our eye of faith turn steadily towards you, patiently waiting in hope for the fulness of your salvation, bearing the pain of evil days, in Jesus of the Cross, who loved his own even to the end, and who kept on trusting even when there was no answer to his cry.

Refrain for Part Three: We trust in the folly of the Cross.

Can we hold now to such faith?
Is God's name an offence to our ears?
Is God deaf to the cry of the child,
offering no relief to the burning of pain,
letting the horror of life run wild,
sitting lofty and high, refusing to act?

So do we argue and wrestle in faith,
fiercely refusing to loosen our hold.
We demand that you listen to whisper and howl,
that your deeds may fulfil your nature and name.

This is our story from Jeremiah and Job,
for we find you obscure and perplexing.
Who are you? Who do you say that you are?
Why must we be buffeted by malice and chance?

Is our cry no more than our pride?
Is our mind too small? Is our eye too dim?
Do not quiet our pain with dazzling display.
The open wound of the child accuses you still.

Is there a cry in the depths of your being,
in the heart and soul of your chosen Christ-Self?
Stretched between earth and the heavens,
we see a striving so awesome,
a strange and harrowing love,
a bearing of pain between father and son,
a loving right through to the end,
through the worst of devil and death.

Truly you are an offence, O God,
and scandalous too are the outcries of faith.
They bite deep into the lines of our faces,
as we strive to be faithful and true.
Keep us from the scandal of hypocrisy,
selfish and faithless, prayers merely mouthed,
so far from the Place of the Skull,
too indifferent to be in conflict with you,
too icily cold for your friendship.

Today if you hear the voice of *this* God,
your heart need no longer be hardened.

O God of the Cross, keep us passionate through our wrestling with your ways, and keep us humble before the mystery of your great love, known to us in the face of Jesus Christ.

*Refrain for Part Four: In the depths of our darkness
you are rising, O Christ.*

And can those who are buried give you worship,
those ground to the dust give you praise?
Will nothing be left but the wind and the silence,
a dead earth, abandoned, forgotten?

But you are a God who creates out of nothing,
you are a God who raises the dead,
you are a God who redeems what is lost,
you are a God who fashions new beauty,
striving with the weight of your glory,
bearing the infinite pain.

The footfalls of faith may drag through our days,
God's gift of a costly and infinite enduring.
We remember your deliverance of your people of old,
we remember the abundance of the earth you have given us,
we remember the care and compassion of folk,
we remember your victory of long-suffering love.

The power of the powers is but a feather in the wind!
Death is transfigured to glory for ever!

Risen Christ, breaking the bonds of death, shine on us with eyes of compassion and glory. Let light flood the dungeons of our rejected and downtrodden selves. So may the oppressed go free, the weak rise up in strength, and the hungry be fed, now in these our days.

IV. EMPTY AND AFRAID, YET TRUSTING

A version of Psalm 56

Refrain: I will put my trust in you, O God,
I will praise you for your Presence.
I will trust and not be afraid:
what can mortal flesh do to me?

THE echo of the infant sounds,
the unwanted child cries for affection,
The giver of my life is my adversary,
persistently pressing upon me.

I feel nothing but hatred towards me,
I stand on no ground of my worth.
Are my tears counted in your flask,
are my hurts noted in your book?

I feel I am dying before I am born,
my feet slip from under me.
Empty and distressed, I am nothing,
yet I yearn for life to the full.

From the midst of my wasteland
of needs never met,
knowing my emptiness,
I wait to be filled.

Rain on the desert of my terror,
fill my empty soul to overflowing,
that I may joy in the life that you give,
a river that will flow to those who are parched.

As Mary opened her will, her heart, and her womb, giving her emptiness to be filled with your living presence, so, Giver of life, encourage us to be empty and needy before you, that, being born in us, your presence may displace all our fear and distress.

V. THE BODY OF GOD

A version of Psalm 79

Refrain: O God, we wound your body:
come quickly, heal and save us.

WE neglect, we ravage the body.
We rape the earth, your temple.
We pollute the rivers, the oceans.
We care not for the soil that sustains us.
And the earth cries out in pain.
The algae fills the creeks,
sucking down the unwary,
releasing its poisonous fumes.

We neglect, we ravage the body.
We take our pleasures with violence.
We forget the language of reverence.
We care not for the weak and the vulnerable.
And the people cry out in pain.
Their anger rises in vengeance:
they pass on the needles infected,
they delight in spreading disease.

We neglect, we ravage the body.
We flatten the beautiful cities.
We ransack the places of prayer.
We care not for beauty, for peace.
And the land cries out in pain.
The contorted ruins smoulder.
The survivors stumble in shock,
their children inherit their wounds.

We neglect, we ravage the body.
Radiation drifts on the wind.
Waste is dumped in the oceans.
We care not for fish or for bird.
And the trees cry out in pain,
sprouting misshapen leaves.
An earthquake in the depths of the seas
splits open the canisters of doom.

O God, forgive our murderous deeds and blind, unthinking rage. Give us your Spirit of compassionate anger, that we may live and work in harmony with you for the healing of the body of this planet, gasping for air, sores weeping on its skin. Make us a people of one earth, loved and cherished as bodies should.

VI. IN BLEAK DESPAIR

A version of Psalm 88

*Refrain: There is drought in the depths of my being,
no rain, no water, no life.*

THE praise of your salvation, O God,
has died on lips that are parched.
The story of your wonders towards us
has turned hollow, bitter, and sour.
I doubt any prayer can enter your heart,
your ear is deaf to my cry.

Soul-deep I am full of troubles,
and my life draws near to the grave.
I totter on the edge of the abyss,
ghostly, ghastly, shrivelled.
I am like the wounded in war that stagger,
like a corpse strewn out on the battlefield.

I belong no more to my people,
I am cut off from your presence, O God.
You have put me in the lowest of dungeons,
in a pit of scurrying rats.
To a wall that drips with water I am chained,
my feet sink into mud.

I feel nothing but a pounding in my head,
surges of pain overwhelm me.
I cannot endure this suffering,
this furious onslaught, so searing.
I can remember no time without terror,
without turmoil and trouble of mind.

I have been dying since the day of my birth:
O God, have I ever really existed?
I have never known who I am,
and even my friends who once loved me,
who gave me some sense of belonging,
have drawn back in horror and left me.

My sight fails me because of my trouble;
there is no light in the place of deep dark.
I am alone, bewildered, and lost;
yet I cannot abandon you, God.
Day after day I cry out to you,
early in the morning I pray in your absence.

Do you work wonders among the tombs?
Shall the dead rise up and praise you?
Will your lovingkindness reach to the grave,
your faithfulness to the place of destruction?
Are the stories of old an illusion?
Will you again do what is right in the land?

*In times of despair, O God, rain showers of gentleness upon us, that we may
be kindly one to another and also to ourselves. Renew in us the spirit of hope.
Even in the depths of the darkness, may we hear the approach of the One who
harrows hell and greets even Judas with a kiss.*

VII. A CALM AUTHORITY

A version of Psalm 93

Refrain: To the chaos that storms, without and within,
speak with assurance, Peace, be still.

IN the silence of the night your word was spoken.
a calm creative word in the heavens.
It was but a whisper of your voice,
the faint rustling of your robes of glory.
Sovereign of the universe, yet did you hide yourself,
so that your light might not shrivel us.

In quiet ways you hold the world together,
chaos contained by your compassionate power.
When the seas hurl their pounding waves,
when the hurricane howls across the ocean,
when the tornado rips through the farmland,
when the rivers rage through city streets,
still do you set a limit to their power,
that they might not overwhelm us for ever.

The surges of chaos pound through our heads,
a murderous fury rises within us;
wrenched apart by the sobbing of grief,
we are lost and bewildered, tossed to and fro.
A relentless pain throbs through our bones,
we scream in the night at the faces of terror.
Yet even as we plunge in the fearful abyss,
the face of the crucified is there in the void.

For where do we best see your power?
Nowhere else but a man who is stricken,
deserted and betrayed by his friends,
killed by his people, an outcast, unclean.
The chaos they dared not face in themselves
they hurled with abuse and the nails.
They hid from their pain in the thicket of laws,
and refused to allow their wounds to be healed.

The material world looked so solid around us,
we never even dreamed of chaos in matter.
As the cloud mushroomed high in the desert,
we were stunned by the force we'd unleashed.
The power of apocalypse is now in our hands:
is the calm word of God lost for ever?

Creator God, you have entered the very fabric of the universe, for ever committed to bringing harmony out of chaos. Assure us of your presence in the midst of our perplexities and fears, that you will endure with us and speak the calm word of a deeper and more lasting peace.

B

Praying with those
who have been violently assaulted
or sexually abused

WHERE violence has been done to the boundary between public and private life, particular care needs to be taken with any healing ritual and prayer that there is a secure boundary which cannot be intruded upon. Where that is so, there can be a measure of healing when a particular deep emotional wound can be exposed for acceptance and binding. Even though a group may be entirely supportive, parts of this process of healing may well need to be undertaken by the person alone or at most with one trusted other. There needs to be sufficient sense of privacy for acknowledgement of the violation and sufficient openness so that the violation may be held and to a degree healed.

The person may already have shared the painful story in a counselling setting. It may be that some of the detail is still too painful to tell out loud. But it may be that the story can be told as part of the ritual, or that it can be written down and presented to the group.

In preparation for the ritual the person may wish to take a cleansing bath and be gently massaged all over the body.

What follows are but suggestions, not experienced by the author directly but entrusted to him by those who have and who believe them to be of help. And such prayer seems, alas, all too sorely needed.

I. THE TRUTH OF OUR FEELINGS

1   THE blood that flows cries for revenge.
2   Cursed be the violence of the strong.
1   The child howls in the lonely night.
2   Cursed be the hand that bruised.
1   The woman/man lies sobbing on the floor.
2   Cursed be the hard eyes and the unyielding stone.
1   The body that trusted lies rigid in shock.
2   Cursed be the relishing of pain.
1   The weak are intimidated and afraid.
2   Cursed be our arrogance and lust for power.
1   The abused shrink away in silent shame.
2   Cursed be the evil power of secrecy.
1   The abusers protest their innocence.
2   Cursed be those who deny their responsibility.
1   The comfortable turn away, refusing to see.
2   Cursed be our collusion and cowardice.

ALL   Just and holy God,
        receive our fear and shame,
        our grief and anger,
        and channel these strong energies
        in the service of truth and healing.

II. THE GREETING OF LOVE AND THE TELLING OF THE STORY

N, we love you, we affirm you, we recognise you.
We hear and see your wounding;
We touch your pain.
Tell us, if you will, your story.

[*N may wish to tell the story or present a written version of it, perhaps with such words as, This is my story. I am wounded and I hurt. If the story has already been told to someone in the group, perhaps such words as these could be used: I have shared my story with X, who has received it with care. I am wounded by what happened to me, and I hurt and seek healing.*]

N, you have been harmed but you have not lost your
   capacity for healing.
You have been helpless but you have not lost your ability
   to act.
You have been humiliated but you have not lost your
   integrity.
You have been violated but you have not lost your strength
   for love.

By the sweep of our arms [*a gesture here of wide dismissal*]
and in the power of the Holy Spirit,
we dispel the forces of violence and abuse,
of harm and humiliation.

By the gathering of our arms [*a gesture here of embrace*]
and in the presence of the Holy Spirit,
we affirm the ultimate power of love and truth and healing.

[*It may be appropriate for the piece of paper to be burned, and some such
words used as these: May the evil and the harm wither away and be
consumed.*]

III. LIGHT IN THE DARK PLACES

N, let the light of this candle be for you the light of God,
as you meet the darkness in the deep places of your being.
See the hidden things, the creatures of your dreams,
the storehouse of forgotten memories,
the gifts you never knew you had been given.
Touch the wellspring of your life,
and hear your own true nature and your own true name.
Take the freedom to grow into that self
the seed of which was planted at your making...

Listen to the language of your wounds.
Do not pine away in the pain of them,
but seek to live from the depths of them.
Make the extent of your desolation
the extent of your realm...

Take into your arms your wounded frightened child within.
Give her/him your adult caring strength,
for your child has protected your gifts
until the time they can be given and not be betrayed...

May your only wounds be these:
the wound we cannot avoid because we belong to one another
and feel and hear the murmur of the world's pain;
the wound of a sense of compassion for others;
the wound of a sense of longing for God,
the source of life and love deep within us and beyond us...

IV. THE ANOINTING

A small empty bowl can be passed round the group, together with a small jug of oil from which each person can pour a little into the bowl. A prayer of blessing can be used, and different members of the group can anoint different parts of the body. The detail needs to be worked out as appropriate to the person concerned. For example,

> *At the anointing of the throat*
> From violence to your voice, be healed.
>
> *At the anointing of hands and feet*
> From violence to your body, be healed.
>
> *At the anointing of the breast*
> From violence to your feelings, be healed.
>
> *At the anointing of the forehead*
> From violence to your mind, be healed.
>
> *At the anointing of the lower stomach*
> From violence to your sexuality, be healed.

V. THE PRAYING

THE Creator Spirit surrounds you,
upholds you on all sides,
flows round you, caresses you, loves you,
and wills you to be whole.

N, be healed.
Be well again.
Live from your scars with compassion.

Love your flesh-body,
You are a body,
not a no-body,
not just any-body,
but some-body.

And we are a body,
the Body of Christ.
The body is the dwelling place
of the healing Holy Spirit.
You are a body in the Spirit.

Be in love with life,
wrestle with the chaos and the pain,
with yourself and with others,
spirit echoing Spirit,
trusting in the victory of the vulnerable,
glimpsing the peace and wholeness, the justice and freedom,
that comes from following the Pioneer
made perfect in suffering,
striving and yearning and crying out
from the very depths and heights
of the world's anguish and the world's bliss,
and so becoming friends and partners of God
in the divine creating.

The God who gives healing to the violated
and power to the powerless,
fill you with the spirit of a strong love,
that you may flow with grace and truth and beauty.

C
What price healing
in a time of epidemic?

What price healing?

Nobody takes pleasure in facing that question. Even to listen to a lecture on this theme demands a certain price – a willingness to look steadily at a phenomenon, both of a disease and of the reactions of a society, that will not go away. Its presence is affecting us all. It is hardly light entertainment. The issue is as wide-ranging and challenging as one that is in many ways similar: What price peace in a time of nuclear power? For it is as frightening to be faced with the facts of invisible radiation as it is with the facts of invisible viruses. The effects of exposure to either may take years to become apparent: when they do, the consequences are deadly. I forget the exact figure, but is it something like ten thousand HIV IIIs that can dance on the top of a pin? And untold thousands of particles of plutonium can be contained in a jamjar.

Here is a quotation from a book called *Microbes and morals* by T. Rosebury (Viking, New York, 1971, p.71): '...a mysterious epidemic, hitherto unknown, which had struck terror into all hearts by the rapidity of its spread, the ravages it made, and the apparent helpless of the physicians to cure it.' So wrote William Osler early this century. He was referring to syphilis in Europe four hundred years ago. Fear grows again, though the quotation, while hardly a comfort, does give us cause to be cautious. Such epidemics and the panics, medical and moral, that accompany them, are not new.

Matter of fact

Nevertheless, the fears are real. And one way of putting them in proportion is simply to be more matter-of-fact. However disturbing the information may be, facts are always more friendly then ignorance and rumour. Fear tends to distort and exaggerate the reality. From leaflets and from television, from the Government and the Terrence Higgins Trust, there is now an abundance of information, even if the inferences drawn and the interpretations made vary wildly. But I wonder how many people will continue to refuse to face facts because they will not pay the price of being disturbed and consequently actually feeling the fears that lurk behind the statistics of disease? I suspect that there is less to be afaid of than the alarmists suppose and more to be cautious of than the complacent believe – particularly those who see no reason to warn the heterosexual population in this country.

Then there is the matter-of-fact, day by day, response of scientists and doctors to a new disease, and of all who care for those who are ill. These are very ordinary men and women shouldering an unexpected extra burden on behalf of the rest of us. I don't suppose it's ever been easy to be introduced at a party as a consultant in sexually transmitted diseases, but how many of the other guests would now be at ease round the cheese fondue? Such doctors pay a price for difficult work, not least because of all that is projected on to them out of other people's irrational fears.

I am also thinking of the dull, boring, and repetitive tasks of the research scientists and laboratory technicians, work that is hardly ever given publicity simply because what is dull, boring, and repetitive has little news value. There is no story until there is a 'breakthrough' – and most of these are false dawns, and the headlines have their little day.

There is the daily unglamorous duty of the round of doctors and nurses and health visitors, a duty which they assume largely without comment, but which is nonetheless costly in terms of time and energy and emotional strain. For one health visitor, her work with two particular patients had felt like being alongside two sons and watching them die within months of each other, just as they had begun to live their adult lives.

There is the calm, consistent caring of charge nurses and counsellors in the face of bewilderment, panic, anger, and, in some, increasing disfigurement and weakness. It is costly to retain such an inner peace that one can find the right words and gestures to defuse an emotionally charged encounter.

I could add others: the Samaritan, who is also no longer news, but who continues patiently and warmly to listen and befriend, and the 'Buddy' of the Terrence Higgins Trust, the one who has volunteered to do everything possible for a person suffering from opportunistic diseases, whether at home or in hospital, especially the ones whose families, friends, and colleagues have refused to bear their share of the cost. For we are talking about the pain-bearers of our society, those who are willing to bear *more* than their fair share.

Albert Camus wrote in a measured and moving way in his novel, *The Plague,* that we learn in times of epidemic that "there are more things to admire in men and women than to despise. (The story) could not be one of final victory. It could be only the record of what had had to be done, and what assuredly would have to be done again... by all who, while unable to be saints but refusing to bow down to pestilence, strive their utmost to be healers."

There is so much small-scale heroism, the thousands of acts of kindness and skill willingly performed by ordinary people who refuse to moralize and who find the only immorality in the suggestion that there might be a heavenly reward for good works done on earth. They simply do what needs to be done for human beings in need.

I suppose there is a further immorality, and that is a refusal to acknowledge our gratitude. For appreciation of what we are already doing is the best way of encouraging us to do more. A retired Archbishop of Canterbury, on hearing of a planned moral campaign by his successor, is reputed to have remarked that general exhortations to be good never have any effect.

At whose expense are you relatively well?

Some years ago, Dr Michael Wilson threw out this challenge: At whose expense are you relatively well? If we try and answer that question in a global perspective, we are forced to realize that we are well and well-fed in this country at the expense of the poor of Africa and Asia.

If we think of the resources of the health service, we have to recognize that somebody has to make hard decisions of choice every day as varying worthy claims are made on those resources – even if, in a more generous political climate, they were to be expanded. How many kidney machines can a health authority (service?) afford if a new ward has to be opened to cope with those who are suffering from a new disease? How much money does a government put into research, how much into treatment, how much into prevention? The questions would take all night to list, let alone to answer, yet some people bear the burden of decisions taken.

Not least does this remind us the costliness of pioneer work of any kind. I was surprised to be told that it costs up to $15,000 a month to treat a premature baby in the technologically most advanced hospital unit in the world, in Colorado Springs in the United States. But I saw in that unit a sonar screening device, costing heaven knows how much, that gave an accurate picture of a baby's internal organs without the need for any invasive techniques like X-rays or optic tubes. Who pays? And who decides the allocation of resources for preventive medicine so that the infant mortality rate in famine-stricken African countries might decrease?

I have no doubt that we want to say Yes to all these possibilities. But that is to be impossibly idealistic. For example, where research into viruses is concerned, it is clear that experiments in genetic engineering are costly enough to deflect resources away from the more obviously and often chronically ill. Yet Sir Donald Acheson (reported in *The Guardian* on 9 March 1987) claims that with the technique of splicing cells we shall in time come up with a vaccine against HIV III. And of course the very existence of the virus would not have been demonstrated without the invention of the electron microscope.

For most of us such research seems like wild science fiction. But we know that without it we would be faced with a disease as mystifying as was bubonic plague in the Middle Ages. *At the same time,* how many sufferers from epidemic and endemic diseases in Central Africa are denied fundamental public health measures such as were the major cause of the dramatic drop in the incidence of such scourges in Britain in the nineteenth century? Whichever way you turn, the answers are difficult. Who pays?

'Monkey business'

It does seem as if it is Africa that pays most. The most common cause of immune deficiency on that continent is malnutrition.

And over the past few years Africa has been blamed for being the place of origin of HIV. It was easy for Europeans and Americans to be seduced by theories of origin for fear of AIDS – dubbed AFRAIDS – affects us even if the virus does not. Where there is confusion and panic, caution and prudence suffer. We want to know exactly where the virus came from so that we can pin the blame on to somebody.

So I remember easily being sold the plausible theory that HIV came from Africa, either from a previously isolated area where it had been endemic and where the population had built up a degree of immunity or from a species of monkey (possibly the green monkey, so the theory went, which may have scratched a human being and passed on the infection). So the virus was supposed to have spread to America and Europe from the heart of the so-called 'dark' continent.

A documentary film on Channel 4 television in January 1990 questioned the hypothesis. For a start, HIV has never been found in any remote area of Africa, nor in an isolated tribe. Then there is no known instance of a retro-virus jumping species. Further, the virus in the green monkey is far too dissimilar to HIV for there to be a connection.

In 1986 there were five papers presented at a congress in Paris disproving the theory. In a laboratory in Germany 7000 serum samples containing a leukaemia virus had been collected between 1970 and 1985 from Africa, Japan, and the Caribbean. No HIV was found in any of them until 1982–3 – after the first cases of AIDS had been reported in the United States. Yet the myth has persisted, with its racist overtones: 'Africans eat monkey... their children play with them...'

A more likely theory, but with no conclusive evidence, is that the virus originated in America. The first cases were noted there in 1981, in Europe in 1982, and not in Africa until 1983. No one knew, for example, that blood banks, donated by America to Africa, might contain the virus.

Further, though retro-viruses do not cross species naturally, they can do so when the biological barrier is broken down – as in gene-splitting. Articles in the magazines *The Lancet, Science,* and *Nature* have stated that HIV *could* have been manufactured by the mid-seventies. Did it escape accidentally from a laboratory? Were volunteers in prisons tested with it and released because there were no symptoms? It is known that a military research programme was mooted, in the late sixties, into a virus that would destroy the immune system: no one knows if it went ahead. Certainly between 1983 and 1988 there was a 500% increase in American research into dangerous pathogens.

It would be easy to build another myth, easy for Africans to say that the West wants to decimate their populations so that empty land can be colonized. But we are faced with the bizarre possibility that millions of pounds have been spent on constructing a virus – only that we should spend millions of pounds learning how to deal with it. What price healing?

Openness about sex and sexuality

I turn to another price that is being paid. It has been quite costly for some people to face, again in a matter-of-fact way, frank and sober talk on television about the physical details of sexual activity. It has always been difficult to let light into dark places of taboo. How much more so when the taboos on sex are added to those on blood, semen, disfigurement, and death. So a pat on the back for the octogenarians who take it all in their stride and say, I wish we'd had some straightforward information in our day. And a round of applause for the elderly woman from Dorset who wrote a letter to say that she would have preferred a free bag of coal from the Government to advice on the use of condoms.

Then there was the subtle but insidious assumption that we could ignore this disease because it would carry off those whose presence in a 'healthy' society was not really wanted, but which would not affect the 'normal' population. So in America it was assumed that there was no need to worry about Hispanic people, black people, people addicted to heroin, poor people, gay people: they have no power, no voice, and are not much use. Even if you do not voice those assumptions, if they are at the back of your mind, it stops you making a protest.

Too many gay men will have paid an unnecessary price because of political complacency, because of a refusal to take the warning signs seriously, and because punitive feelings are too easily evoked from our unconscious minds whenever we feel threatened. To be a member of a rejected minority, with all the consequent internalizing of hatred, makes a person all the more liable to stress and breakdown, whether emotionally or physically. Somebody made the comparison between gay men in American cities and the canaries that used to be taken down coal mines: if they stopped singing and died, the miners were warned of the presence of lethal gas. The more vulnerable always suffer first.

It is also ironic that the 'safe-sex' campaign is needed least by the openly gay man, who has most probably been taking precautions anyway over the last few years (the incidence of other sexually transmitted diseases among gay men has dropped considerably). The advice is more difficult to heed if you feel forced by others' hostility to be furtive and anonymous in the expression of your sexuality.

Too many people are still – and, with the fear whipped up by some newspapers, increasingly – afraid of what their families, friends, and fellow-workers will say and do if it becomes known that they are gay. Can we face the price of healing that is an open acceptance of the equal worth of a gay person? Can gay people who are secretive face the price of being more open? Can the guardians of our society, not least the churches, take the opportunity of encouraging the formation and sustaining of stable same-sex relationships?

Incidentally, the drive to control gonorrhoea and syphilis in the nineteenth century had little impact on the containment of the disease. Strong measures were taken against prostitutes, including forced medical examination in publicly known centres, at the entrances to which they were often vilified by the crowds who had come to gloat. Similar legal constraints were introduced in the First World War against women who infected soldiers. Notice that it was the women who were treated as criminals, not the men.

No, the decline in the incidence of these diseases came with improved medical treatment, together with a new confidentiality in clinics, and the improved position of women both socially and economically, with fewer women finding themselves with no seeming alternative but to go on the streets to make even the smallest of livings. If people are valued and respected for who they are, they are less likely to put themselves in the way of infection. Women and gay men are still involved in that struggle.

Let me add that I am *not* saying that gay men are simply the victims of 'bad luck'. The syndrome of 'There's nothing wrong with us' can affect the militant libertarian as much as the religious fundamentalist. (Perhaps both need to discover the delights of laughter and of making love!) Certainly in the early days of the disease there was an element of misfortune through lack of knowledge. But it is not anti-gay to say that certain patterns of behaviour can make a virus deadly. And to say it again, those patterns of behaviour can be and have been changed: sheer prudence indicates that there should be no exchange of body fluids between two people if there is any *reason* (and I stress the word 'reason', so irrational has been much of the reaction to this syndrome), to suppose that one or other is infected with a potentially lethal virus.

Eros re-visited

Let us take this issue further, from the point of view of those who actually do carry the virus. Through sexual relationships human beings seek an intimate exchange of their whole beings, including affection and pleasure, a measure of healing of old emotional wounds, not least an affirmation of basic worth by another human being, and a creative triggering of something beyond themselves: for most people this means the procreation and nurture of children, and for everybody it can mean an increased maturity and creativity in the rest of life. Even sexually transmitted diseases do not banish all possibility of intimacy, of affection and pleasure, of healing and creativity, in a relationship that is broadly erotic, and may, within limits, be specifically sexual. After all, human beings are fairly ingenious in these matters.

What *is* precluded if you carry a dangerous virus is the kind of activity that involves penetration and procreation. One immediate reaction is to ask what other options are there? A leap of imagination may be difficult for the macho male, but what, for example, of genital masage for the disabled, of sexual stimulation in a lesbian relationship? Such imagination is not easy if you have been conditioned to understand sex as mechanical and incidental. And a traditional approach to sex, from the point of view of men in power, is one of penetration and procreation, the man dominant over the woman.

For centuries the official teaching of the Roman Catholic Church has been that every sexual act must be open to conception. A recent illustration of this principle was the permission to use a condom for the purpose of artificial insemination provided a slight perforation kept open the possibility of conception by 'natural' means.

With imagination, sexual energy might be re-directed to serve deeper levels of healing, no longer with associations of ritual performance, dominance, children and the inheritance of property, but with those subtler associations of mutuality, intimacy, healing, and creativity. Heterosexual couples and gay men have much to learn from a group about whose sexual activity little is generally known and who are least at risk from HIV infection – lesbian women. Questions about that will have to be asked in a humble not lascivious way: there is some costly repenting to be done first.

Such thoughts may also enable us to take opportunities for a more relaxed eroticism – a spreading throughout the flesh-and-blood body of pleasurable sensations, a slower rhythm about which again women may have much to teach men. Sexual relationships *could* become less harsh and exploitative, more caring, where there would be no force or intimidation, nor any activity that belied the meaning of that relationship or obstructed the sharing of affection, pleasure, healing, creativity. I wonder how many physically healthy people will pay the price of giving up old assumptions, yet finding in the process an enrichment of the whole range of their erotic activity. And the cost for the virus carrier is this: How can I *now* draw near to the one I love in such a way that, in these given circumstances, more love is made between us?

I do not understand why Christopher Booker (I think it was in the *Daily Telegraph*) has to interpret all gay sexuality in terms of soulless activities, but he has part of the truth when he says,'....the central thread of health and stability in human society has lain in selfless love, the sustaining of life, and the procreation and nurture of children.' Surely the ideas I've been exploring can be included in that. For sexuality *does* have a great deal to do with pleasure, and such pleasure has been thought of, even in the much-maligned Christian tradition, as one of the best analogies for far greater and more full-bodied and full-bloodied pleasure in the life to come, indeed is an anticipation of that life. There may be a price to pay in time of epidemic, but it is not to be pinned down in agony for ever.

Emotional responses to disease

If it is disturbing to face both the details of sexual behaviour and our perspectives on sexual relationships, how much more difficult it is when a person who is dearly loved begins to show symptoms of acquired immune deficiency. If your spouse or lover or offspring or best friend told you tonight that they had developed signs of the skin cancer, Kaposi's Sarcoma, what would your reaction be?

Suddenly, in a very clear light, your attitudes would be shown for what they are, at an emotional level beneath that of rational discussion. The degree of your own deeper health would be revealed by your response, in terms both of deeds and of unresolved feelings. We do not of course always act on those first feelings, but there will be dis-ease between us which needs to be acknowledged and worked on.

I remember Donald Nicholl once observing that if our reaction to anything awful happening to another person is that he or she deserves it, our hearts are cold and hateful. For we have demonized the other and deadened our compassion. We may feel more comfortable with ourselves, but it is a false peace.

It is easy to be trapped in an endless to and fro of blaming. I mean, you could say that the spread of HIV in the population at large is a punishment of heterosexual people for being anti-gay (that is, wicked), and homophobic (that is, irrationally afraid in an exaggerated manner, and therefore mentally ill). They gave too little too late of money for research, of support for same-sex relationships, and of welcome for those who had been cast out. The Roman Catholic Archbishop of New York, one of the more conservative of the American hierarchy, was lampooned in the gay press by the headline, 'Cardinal O'Connor causes AIDS.'

It is even easier to project the blaming on to God, and to talk glibly about the wrath of God against gay people, as if a disease were divine retribution from on high, and as if God rejoiced at lethal diseases and was petulantly disappointed when headway was made against cancers and heart disorders, and as if he were especially sparing of lesbian women...

In any case it is sounder in biblical terms to think of the judgment of nations more than of individuals. And if God judges nations by means of disease, why does not every Western European have AIDS? For the biblical witness is to the seriousness, not of sexual sins but of a refusal to help the poor.

It is much more helpful to accept that the question of disease and responsibility is complex. We can say only this, that we all have some measure of choice in the way we conduct our lives, and we all have to bear the consequences of calculated risks. I mean, just how many cream teas is it safe to consume in Devon each summer? This applies to *all of us,* and we are all caught up in the disagreeable fact that nothing in this life turns out completely and permanently well. There is no room for singling out a particular disease or a group of people, sealing them off and condemning them. If no one is an island, well, there is no island to which exiles can be sent.

Social costs

But what is happening to us as a community, as a society of people who are bound up together? Awareness of a virus begins to pervade everything, just as nuclear and ecological awareness does, somehow reflecting the character of the times we live in, not least because the very cohesiveness of the organism is at risk – the disintegration of the flesh-body at the cellular level, the erosion of trust in day-to-day relationships, the strain on the resources of nations and planet. And it is true that if AIDS increasingly affects people in young to middle life there are bound to be disturbing and costly economic and social implications.

It *may* be that I am being bewitched by my own fears and by the fears of government and media, and there is some evidence that the rate of increase of new cases is less than was expected a few years ago. But no wonder that people are borrowing a technically religious word to refer to what is happening as apocalyptic. Together with the nuclear and ecological issues, it is probable that the price of our healing will be an upheaval the like of which has few if any historical parallels. It feels as if we are living through an end-time, which also may be a beginning-time. Death-throes or birth-pangs? I suppose it depends on whether or not you have hope. But in such times you need a steady nerve, rational responses in policy-making, resilience, trust, humour – qualities that are hard to sustain but vital to our survival. If we adopt the phrase 'survival of the fittest', what kind of person will be best fitted to survive? The species white-macho-male may be the one that finds adaptation to the new conditions the most painful.

In search of meaning – Metaphors of illness
I may be falling prey to another temptation, to import meaning into these things prematurely. It is certainly a religious temptation. We want to make sense of what is happening, and it is all too easy for moral and religious metaphors to cluster round a phenomenon that mystifies us. Susan Sonntag in her essay *Illness and metaphor* (1978; Penguin 1983) has shown how this happened in the past with tuberculosis. TB raised similar feelings of dread to AIDS. Sonntag quotes Kafka who was dying from TB in 1924 and reported that 'everybody drops into a shy, evasive, glassy-eyed manner of speech.' (p.11) By contrast I remember the matter-of-fact way in which I received the news that a friend of mine had contracted TB in the early sixties and had to be in hospital for a while. I was a little envious of the medical advice he was later given to find a job by the sea.

Over the past decades it has been a different disease that has provoked dread and whispers. People have died 'after a long illness' and the obituary notice does not specify the kind of cancer. It is as if the very name is felt to be contagious, let alone the sufferer. To be diagnosed and labelled is to be damned – a sentence of death, if not of hell.

So we find people of every generation scapegoated and blamed for their illness, with a condemning God waiting in the wings. Is it not strange therefore that we are far less blaming of businessmen for their heart disease, passing lightly over the possibility that eating certain foods in certain quantities and working in certain stressful ways may not have exactly helped their state of health? I am by no means suggesting we ought to switch our blaming on to them, nor a direct cause and effect. I am simply noticing that in practice we discriminate among diseases, and that where the business world is concerned men and women are making a lot of money there by dint of very hard work – two of the idols of our time.

Cancer on the other hand seems almost obscene: a very private matter not to be talked about in public. It is only as it becomes less mystifying, more susceptible to cure, that we are beginning to be able to talk more openly about it.

With TB, people used metaphors of 'consumption', of being burned up, while with cancer the metaphors are military. Alien cells invade and multiply, blocking healthy bodily functions, and extending their territory to take over and destroy. And whereas TB was thought to be associated with too much romantic passion – consumed by ardour – cancer has been thought to be associated with inhibited passion, whether of sexuality or of anger.

Condemnation is never far from our reaction to diseases, at least for as long as there is no cure. How much more so now with a disease that so far affected groups of people whom so many tend to think are getting their just deserts through what is perceived as a misuse of drugs or sex. Add to that the perception about infected blood, the very life-carrier itself, and the action of a very specific virus, fragile and hard to catch, becomes loaded with an incredible amount of feeling, metaphor, and interpretation that have very little to do with any actual medical conditon. A vulnerable, very ill, and often dying person is further devastated by these punitive reactions that wish at best to isolate and at worst to be violently cruel.

Stress and fragility

I suspect that one reason behind this violence is our renewed sense of fragility as a species, not only our vulnerability to radiation and pollution and to a virus carried by blood and semen, but our uncertainty with one another on occasions of intimacy. We are confused, to say the least. The old boundaries have not yet been replaced with commonly accepted new ones.

Add to this the fact of our continual bombardment with information which is difficult to digest, but which we allow to intrude into our homes via the television.

The American writer May Sarton mused in her journal for 18 November 1974: "I am more and more convinced that in the life of civilizations as in the lives of individuals too much matter that cannot be digested, too much experience that has not been *imagined* and probed and understood, ends in total rejection of everything – ends in anomie. The structures break down and there is nothing to 'hold onto'." (*The house by the sea,* Norton, New York, 1977, 1981, p. 25)

We find ourselves forced to cope with relationships with a greater variety of people than did our ancestors in their more or less self-contained communities. A late twentieth century urban vicar is more liable to burnout than his rural predecessor a hundred years ago. We have to ask ourselves how we relate to neighbours of different cultures, religions, sexualities. We cannot control what happens to our organism's fragile balance when we travel widely and work with many different people. Are new diseases revealing to us the unwelcome truth that we are far more vulnerable than we like to think, and that being so vulnerable means that many will fall by the wayside and that a few will survive with a new wisdom?

Shifts in understanding

The trouble is that we find it all too congenial to label as impure or unclean or sinful those conditions and people whom we are afraid to be near. We want to distance ourselves. Do I draw back ever so slightly from the person next to me who has ordered a dishful of snails in a restaurant? More seriously, we can suddenly find we want to put a lot of ground between ourselves and 'him' or 'her' or 'them'. An irrational urge wells up within us, an urge to banish, and, in the extreme, to destroy. No one is immune from this deficiency.

I notice that in visualization exercises suggested for carriers of HIV, it is military metaphors that are used. For example: imagine that your helper cells are well-armed soldiers with laser weapons zapping the virus, or as little creatures in computer games that gobble up invaders.

What about some alternatives? I read that doctors are now talking more easily about immune *competence* than of immune defences – an ability to perform a task. I hear about the 'splicing' of cells, a word we usually come across in connection with rope and plants and married couples – to make them stronger. I recognize that I am already a 'host' to a number of entities that could get out of hand if a delicate set of checks and balances were to be disturbed. Perhaps we need to learn how to be more compassionate and cunning hosts. If a virus 'hooks into' a cell, could one of the 'helpers' be visualized as 'unhooking' it? It is kindlier thus to think of unpicking the threads: the wool can be used in new ways.

I speculate and I do not wish to mock. I take Susan Sonntag's strictures seriously. But I explore in order to stimulate my own and others' imaginations. Our unexamined metaphors and assumptions could be leading us astray. Might it just be that viruses could be encouraged to mutate into harmless forms, gently as it were helped out of harm's way? Could they somehow be enclosed and transformed? Is it futile anyway to suppose that anything that is destructive can ever be totally destroyed? Perhaps it can be re-arranged.

William Haseltine of Harvard University at the American Association for the Advancement of Science in New Orleans early in 1990 put forward the possibility of a genetically modified version of HIV acting as "a sort of biological guided weapon to seek out and destroy natural HIV." (*The Independent,* 19 February 1990) The military metaphor is again interesting, as are the questions begged by the word 'natural'. But the idea is that the 'weapon' would act by removing the genes that cause the disease and replacing them with a set of genes that would interfere with the working of the entire virus, combating it within the cells of the host. Does the 'host' that is the larger organism, seek to contain and transform unwanted 'guests'?

Suppose that each of us is a universe in miniature. If we banish something, we cannot banish it outside ourselves. Everything within us is deeply interconnected and we cannot cause harm in one place without affecting another. Everything exists by courtesy of everything else. Suppose this is also true of all human beings, and between human beings and other forms of life in the universe beyond the dimensions of time and space of which we are so far aware. Suppose we are all deeply and irrevocably interconnected. And further suppose that we are 'open systems', with an inbuilt ability to change. Then there is a certain *place* for viruses. True, in a universe far from whole, all kinds of people and things will be in the wrong place at the wrong time, but each may have a place, even 'Satan'.

Further suppose that everything is in movement, and that the thrust of that movement is not aimless but is towards health and beauty and harmony. Then there is a place for the suffering that seems inevitably to be part of that process for everybody. But we would then realize that we know and experience it together. We are co-sufferers and we cannot detach ourselves from the process. And a dying and transformation may be part of it all too, for all of us.

Compassion and self-sacrifice

If these things are so, and if we follow the direction of these thoughts a little further, then compassion and self-sacrifice are the only values worthy living by. We may still talk of judgment – in the sense of discernment, of a justice that puts things right and people in a right relationship with one another, in their right space. Condemnation is incompatible, for it separates, even tries to do so finally and utterly, putting people in the wrong place for ever.

More mundanely, the urge to separate is a refusal to be identified with another human being. In Christian faith, Incarnation is about the creative personhood and nature and activity of God being identified with human beings to the point of the worst that can happen. There is startling truth in the headline, 'Christ has AIDS.' Ken Leech has pointed out that "to believe in the Incarnation is to be willing to be contaminated. Sexuality and politics are about imperfection, vulnerability, incompleteness, struggle." (From a paper given in America in 1986, *The AIDS crisis and pastoral care.*)

If that be true, then we need the kind of judgment that would purge us of that tendency to separate ourselves from other people in a superior way, the often surprising upsurge of a desire to be cruel or malicious, the refusal to draw close.

If through our own folly or misfortune or ignorance we find we suffer more than seems fair, we shall not be persuaded to change our ways by threat of thunderbolts. But if somebody draws alongside us in compassion, sacrificing pride and time, unafraid of being, in the world's eyes, contaminated, if we recognize that a cost has been willingly paid out of love for us, however useless we may feel, and however hating of ourselves we have become, then we may cry the tears of relief that we have been recognized as human and as of worth, and the tears of repentance that mean we turn around, and, far from wallowing in self-pity, become willing to bear more for others in a universe where we all belong together. It is our home, and finally we may realize that and indeed come home.

This is at-one-ment at work, that ever-renewed process which Christians see vividly and definitively at work in a crucified outcast, and recognize the sheer costly love of that Spirit that moves through all things that are coming to be. There is no other kind of God than that.

"In the Gospel according to John, Jesus is recorded as saying that it was *not* because of either personal or parental sins that a man had been born blind, but so that God's glory might be shown through him. Is there any way that can be said of the person with AIDS? It sounds preposterous. But I wonder. At times of deep crisis, it does seem that some people have to sacrifice more than they would choose to do – on behalf of others. This is an interpretation that cannot be forced on anyone, but some might choose to accept it.

"May it be that some people, symbolically suffering the universal death we all fear, will be able to help us look that death more clearly in the face, feel the fear, allow it to melt inside us, and so let it become a power of love and will for making some sacrifices of our own, for the sake of the earth's well-being – sacrifices of time and energy and wealth – so that this world may come through the death-throes of an old order and the birth-pangs of a new?" (Adapted by the author from his address, *The other country*, Gay Christian Movement, 1985).

Maybe so, Certainly this: fragile and vulnerable, we all stand in need of compassion. Look into the eyes of the sufferer and see there the grief, fear, pleading, courage, anger, resignation, hope: how can you not show compassion? Will this disease bring forth in us a new tenderness, a willingness to pay the price of healing that is to suffer-with, especially with those we are tempted to despise? That was the whole point of the parable of the Good Samaritan. The correct lawyer was given the example of the one who, as a good Jew of that time, he would most deeply despise, a Samaritan. Follow the example of those you reject. Being kind in a crisis is one thing – but to be shown up for not doing enough by someone you loathe... But we are to give each and all the respect that is the birthright of being human. Let the ones without fault or failure do the condemning.

And being weak does not mean the end of our influence. Accepting that for now we may be a weak spot may mean that we can allow that powerless place to become the exact point through which mercy can flow into our lives and into the lives of those with whom we have to do. Sometimes it is the very obstacles that we cannot get rid of in ourselves that, accepted and pressed into gently, become the places where others find their healing. If they sense that we know deeply the trials of suffering and dying, they will beat a path to our door, and we may both find a deeper healing, in a wondrously strange exchange. We shall have become 'priests' in the only sense of the word that matters, living at the centre of sacrifice, the utter giving upon which the world depends for everything.